ENDORSEMENTS

I like books that say it straight, say it quick and keep my attention. *The ABC's of Leadership* is just such a book. This book will help you as you help others in their leadership journey.

SAMUEL CHAND
Leadership Consultant
Author, Leadership Pain: The Classroom for Growth
(www.samchand.com)
Stockbridge, Georgia

Dr. P. Ronald Wilder knows good leaders must master the basics in order to build a strong foundation for all God calls them to achieve. In his book, *The ABC's of Leadership*, Dr. Wilder uses the alphabets to present the essentials necessary for anyone who wants to grow and to thrive as a leader. Now is the time to take your leadership to another level.

CHRIS HODGES
Senior Pastor, Church of the Highlands
Author, Fresh Air and Four Cups
Birmingham, Alabama

Dr. P. Ronald Wilder weaves his practical leadership gifts as a pastor, teacher, and leader together in this excellent resource regarding leadership. You will often refer to this topically arranged book for insightful ideas drawn from the life experiences of others, saving you hours of study. It will not stay on your library shelf.

DR. GARNET PIKE
President
Spirit Life Ministries International
Oklahoma City, Oklahoma

"Adversity is not popular and certainly not always welcomed when it arrives in the life of a leader. However, it is absolutely necessary toward the development and growth of a leader." (P. Ronald Wilder; *The ABC's of Leadership*)

I am so happy that Dr. Wilder began his book on leadership with this statement. It is a much overlooked aspect of leadership. The outstanding footnotes that I grew to appreciate in reading his exposition on leadership were: 1) leaders are constantly evolving, 2) styles are in constant flux and development, 3) there are no fixed methods and applications in leadership today, and 4) personal attention is required of individuals who desire skill upgrades. Resources, such as this book on leadership, must be seriously considered by those desiring to make their leadership skills better.

The ABC's of Leadership will guide you through the matrix of leadership, analyzing as you traverse the rough terrain of the vast territory called leadership, into your own expression and emphasis. Thank you for your excellent presentation. I thoroughly recommend this masterful work for churches, pastors, leaders, businesses and organizations seeking to upgrade their level of service to humanity.

DR. EARL JOHNSON
Team Leader
According To Pattern Apostolic Care Team
Upland, California

There are numerous books on leadership that are good but this book is simply great! It is written from the heart of an authentic leader who lives out these principles every day. Listen and learn from my good friend, Dr. P. Ronald Wilder, and I promise you that your life and leadership will never be the same.

LEE JENKINS
Senior Pastor, Eagles Nest Church
Author & Speaker
Roswell, GA

Dr. P. Ronald Wilder's work, *The ABC of Leadership*, is a well thought out and profound work. This work certainly lives up to the saying, "Bring the hay down off the high loft so the horses can eat it." His explanations are profound, understandable, detailed, and workable. As a pastor/teacher for thirty-years, I appreciate his approach to teaching. As an author, I appreciate the extensive work he put into this book, which becomes apparent when one reads it. While Dr. Wilder quotes many other leaders in his book, he adds a freshness in his interpretation. I predict upon distribution of this book that he also will be widely quoted. I highly recommend *The ABC's of Leadership* to all current and future leaders.

JAMES C. BLOCKER
Senior Pastor, Maranatha Tabernacle
Author & Teacher
Jamaica, NY

Dr. P. Ronald Wilder is a man of great insight and wisdom especially in matters pertaining to leadership and the church. This book, *The ABC's of Leadership* is a must read for those who are called to lead in any capacity. The first chapter captures your attention and provokes you to evaluate your personal approach of leading others, while first and foremost fine tuning yourself. If this book was available to me years ago, I could have avoided or better handled some of the issues that come with leading people in ministry.

Bishop Sam Thomas
Senior Pastor, Statesville Covenant Cathedral
Teacher & Counselor
Statesville, NC

THE
ABC'S
OF
LEADERSHIP

PRINCIPLES FOR PERSONAL DEVELOPMENT

P. Ronald Wilder

WESTBOW
PRESS®
A DIVISION OF THOMAS NELSON
& ZONDERVAN

Unless otherwise indicated, all Scripture quotations are taken from the *New
American Standard Bible®*, Copyright © 1960, 1962, 1963, 1968, 1971, 1972,
1973, 1975, 1977, 1995 by The Lockman Foundation. Used by permission.

Scripture quotations marked *KJV* are from the *King James
Version* of the Bible. Copyright © 1979, 1980, 1982 by
Thomas Nelson, Inc., publishers. Used by permission.

Scripture quotations marked (NLT) are taken from the Holy Bible,
New Living Translation, copyright © 1996, 2004, 2007 by Tyndale
House Foundation. Used by permission of Tyndale House Publishers,
Inc., Carol Stream, Illinois 60188. All rights reserved.

WestBow Press books may be ordered through booksellers or by contacting:

WestBow Press
A Division of Thomas Nelson & Zondervan
1663 Liberty Drive
Bloomington, IN 47403
www.westbowpress.com
1 (866) 928-1240

ISBN: 978-1-4908-8352-6 (sc)
ISBN: 978-1-4908-8353-3 (hc)
ISBN: 978-1-4908-8351-9 (e)

Library of Congress Control Number: 2015909152

Print information available on the last page.

WestBow Press rev. date: 08/18/2015

Dedication

This book is dedicated to my beautiful and lovely wife, Angela. Thank you for believing in me and continuing to push and encourage me throughout the completion of this book. For the many hours that you prayed for me, your words of encouragement were the fuel needed to keep me going during this project. I thank God for you every day. I love you far beyond what words can describe.

Contents

Preface

In April of 1994, I attended a pastor's conference in Anderson, Indiana. The conference was conducted by John Maxwell. At that time, Maxwell was the senior pastor of Skyline Wesleyan Church in San Diego, California. During the conference, Maxwell said something that changed my life and put me on the course of being a student and teacher of leadership. He said that you would become an expert in any field within five years if you are willing to devote one hour a day to studying that field. Upon hearing what Maxwell said, I determined to become an expert in the field of leadership. I made a commitment to devote one hour each day for the next five years to the study of leadership.

Upon returning home, I began my quest. I began to read leadership books, leadership articles, listen to leadership audio tapes and CD's, and I signed up to receive Maxwell's monthly leadership lessons called INJOY Life Club. Each day, for one hour, I engrossed myself in one or more of these studies of leadership. Many days, I put in more than one hour. Some days it was two, three, or even four hours.

In April of 1999, five years had passed. Every day since that day in April of 1994, I had devoted at least one hour to some aspect of leadership. I was faithful to my commitment and did not miss one single day. So, according to Maxwell, I was now an expert on the subject of leadership. At this point, I chose not to relax. Although I had reached my goal, I determined to continue the one hour-a-day program to learn as much as I could about leadership and to become the best student and teacher of leadership that I could be. I wasn't satisfied with just being a leadership expert; I wanted to be a leadership guru. I wanted to be the very best on the subject of leadership that was humanly possible for me.

So here I am at the writing of the preface to this book in January of 2014, three months shy of twenty years since I made that decision in Anderson, Indiana. Each day for the past twenty years, I have devoted at least one hour to some aspect of leadership. The journey has been incredible and I have learned so many things. I studied behind some of the foremost leadership experts in the United States (both spiritual and secular). While in graduate school at Southwestern Christian University in Bethany, Oklahoma, from 2000 to 2002, I had the privilege of having Dr. J. Robert Clinton as one of my professors. His teachings and perspectives on leadership had a profound impact on my life. I would have to say that on my journey, along with John Maxwell, he was my favorite leadership teacher and expert. I have become what he calls, "a lifelong learner."

My life has been so affected by leadership that I see everything from a leadership perspective. When I look at a movie, I look for the leadership principles in the movie. When watching or attending a sporting event, I observe the coach's leadership and the team captain's leadership. I'm always looking for leadership, whether it's the president of the United States, the CEO of a Fortune 500 Company, the pastor of a local church, a military general, or even a husband and father. I admire leadership in action.

During my journey, I have learned to appreciate leadership. I have discovered two very important things on this journey. First, all leadership is not good leadership; however, bad leadership is more preferable than no leadership. Secondly,

John Maxwell is correct when he says, "Everything rises or falls on leadership." As I have shared my insights with friends and colleagues and conducted leadership seminars in churches across America, I have been encouraged by them to put my knowledge in a book on leadership. This book, *The ABC's of Leadership* is a compilation of many of the things I have learned during my journey.

In writing *The ABC's of Leadership*, I used the masculine pronouns he, him, and his in referring to leaders. This by no means should be interpreted that I believe all leadership is male leadership. I have enormous respect for the many females in leadership who are leading businesses, companies, organizations, schools, colleges, states, cities, churches, ministries, etc. In every place where those masculine pronouns are used, it could equally apply to female leadership. It was less complicated for me to write in a singular gender than a dual gender. Please keep this in mind as you read this book. My intent is not offend or alienate anyone.

Acknowledgments

I owe an exceeding debt of gratitude to the following people who have influenced my ministry and impacted my life:

To Pastor Dana Holmes, you were my first mentor and the one who taught me the ways of God and planted in me the first seeds to becoming a leader in the Kingdom of God. It was you who laid the foundation for ministry that I still wield to this day.

To Bishop Flynn Johnson, you called forth the leader in me and provided the resources and training that enabled me to become the leader that I am today. You gave me the opportunity to touch and walk with giants.

To Bishop Wiley Jackson, you forced me out of my comfort zone. You challenged me to think large and to step out into the deep. You introduced me to leadership and ministry at the next level.

To Bishop Theo Bailey, Bishop Sam Thomas, Pastor Chris Evans and Pastor E. Jonathan Thomas, you guys are four of the best friends that any man could have. You guys have been a great inspiration to me through the years. You have held me accountable and spoken the truth to me in love. But most of all you have believed in me and have allowed me to hone my leadership skills with your congregations. This book would not be without your handprints on my life.

To Dr. Garnet Pike, thank you for giving me the opportunity to further my studies and develop my leadership portfolio at Southwestern Christian University. Your words, "Leaders Lead" have become a hallmark in my life.

Finally, to the Covenant Church International family, thank you for allowing me to be your leader and for the commitment to follow my leadership all these years. You were my first students. You allowed me to make all my mistakes on you and work out all the kinks. I am eternally grateful to God for your support and your loyalty.

Introduction

What is leadership? There is no universally accepted definition of leadership. Ask ten leadership experts to give their definitions and you will probably get ten different answers. How is this possible? This is possible because leadership is an art. The debate continues among the experts regarding whether leadership is an art or a science. I believe that leadership is an art that involves science. Let us look at some different definitions of leadership by some of the leading experts:

- *"Leadership is ... doing the right things."* (Warren Bennis and Burt Nanus)
- *"Leadership is getting others to want to do something that you are convinced should be done."* (Vance Packard)
- *"Leadership is influence."* (John Maxwell)
- *"Leadership is mobilizing others toward a goal shared by the leader and followers."* (Garry Willis)
- *"Leadership is being out front setting the pace."* (P. Ronald Wilder)

Because leadership is an art, it cannot be locked down into one definition. If it were just a science, it could be locked down to a single definition. There is no perfect formula for leadership. Leadership requires skills and a mindset that entails thinking and acting in the moment as well as the ability to convince people to follow you where you want to go. Leadership is fluid, it is ever changing and it is ever evolving.

Leaders lead according to the circumstances and situations they face. What is right and proper in one situation may not be right and proper in another situation. This is the reason we see different leaders react differently to situations. As the world has changed and the cultural mindsets have shifted, leaders have had to adjust the way they lead. The heavy-handed authoritarian leadership, where the leader leads with an iron hand without any input from the followers, has had to give way to servant leadership, where the leader helps the followers to achieve and improve with input from the followers.

Although the art of leadership is constantly evolving, the principles of leadership remain constant and stable. It doesn't matter the circumstances or situations, the principles of leadership are the same. A principle is a fundamental truth. The fundamental truths of leadership never change nor have they changed since the origin of leadership. The shelves of bookstores are filled with good books on the art and even some on the science of leadership. Many well-qualified authors have written extensively on the subject of the art and science of leadership. However, this book, *The ABC's of Leadership* does not deal with the art and science of leadership; it deals with the principles of leadership. It covers the fundamental truths that every leader must embrace in order to be successful and effective as a leader.

The principles of leadership are non-negotiable and cannot be compromised. This book will challenge you and stir you to become a principled leader whose life is guided by the principles written therein. What *The ABC's of Leadership* does is take words beginning with letters of the alphabet and writes about them from a leadership perspective. A leader will find them invaluable to his leadership development. This book does not attempt to use every alphabet nor claim to have covered every principle of leadership. What this book does claim is to equip every serious student of leadership with nuggets that will enhance their growth as a leader and the foundation upon which they can begin to build a legacy of successful leadership. Anyone can become an average leader and many can become good leaders, but only a few ever reach the status of being great leaders. *The ABC's of Leadership* is about greatness. It will plant the seeds of greatness in you as a leader. As you begin to nourish and fertilize those seeds, the inevitable result is that you will become a great leader. I want to encourage you to read through this book over and over and to live with it until the principles in it become second nature to you. When this happens, you will be on your way to becoming what every organization, business, company, church, and family needs...a great leader.

There is an African proverb that says, "Every morning in Africa, a gazelle wakes up. It knows it must run faster than the fastest lion or it will be killed. Every morning a lion wakes up. It knows it must outrun the slowest gazelle or it will starve to death. It doesn't matter whether you are a lion or a gazelle... when the sun comes up, you'd better be running." It is my prayer that after reading this book you, will hit the ground running to become the best leader you can be. Enjoy the journey.

1

Adversity

"The man who is swimming against the stream knows the strength of it."
—Woodrow Wilson

"If we had no winter, the spring would not be so pleasant; if we had not sometimes tasted the adversity, prosperity would not be so welcome."
—Anne Bradstreet

"Adversity has the effect of eliciting talents which, in prosperous circumstances, would have lain dormant."
—Horace

"There is no education like adversity."
—Benjamin Disraeli

The dictionary defines adversity as a state of hardship or affliction, misfortune, or a calamitous event. Adversity is something that all leaders must face from time-to-time in their lives and in their leadership tenure. Adversity is not popular and certainly not always welcome when it arrives in the life of a leader. However, it is absolutely necessary in the development and growth of a leader.

Adversity calls forth and summons the best gifts, the highest talents, and the deepest inner strength a leader possesses. Of all the things that test a leader, nothing tests his commitment, his resolve, and his tenacity like adversity. The manner in which a leader deals with adversity will determine the depth and effectiveness of his leadership. Some leaders collapse under the weight of pressure and adversity while others thrive. This begs the question, is this ability to handle adversity a trait that a leader is born with, or can it be taught? And if it can be taught, is there a formula to improving one's skill of handling adversity? It is both. It is a trait that certain leaders are born with, whereas others are not. However, it can be taught and developed over time.

Overcoming adversity and dealing with setbacks is one of the most important skills a leader can develop. When the organization faces adversity, the leader must skillfully chart the organization through the rough waters. In adverse times, everyone looks to the leader for strength, encouragement and guidance. They look for inspirational leadership. This puts a tremendous burden on the leader in that he doesn't have the luxury of showing weakness, discouragement or loss of focus. During adversity, a leader must become a dealer of hope to those following him, however, this does not mean that you ignore the reality of the situation, but simply, that your attitude is one that illustrates the ability to overcome and be better after the obstacle is over. While facing adversity, a leader must look for keys to assist him through the process. The following steps will help you handle adversity and come out on top:

- **See the situation as temporary and not permanent.** When facing adversity, it seems as if the obstacles will never end, but remember the old saying, "This too shall pass." Sunshine always follows the rain.
- **Approach it as a challenge.** When facing a challenge in sports, the coach tells his team that it is gut-check time. This means it's time to look deep within and find the resolve to overcome the adversity. It's when the leader summons his inner strength. Adversity is a leader's gut-check time.
- **Focus on what you can control.** The things that you can control are your emotions, your attitude, and your focus. In adversity, it is more important what happens in you than what happens around you.
- **Respond with positive action.** Don't sit and wait for something to happen that might change things, but rather make something happen to change things. In other words, be proactive rather than reactive.
- **Call in the troops.** Don't face it alone. Bring in key friends, associates and relationships that will be a source of strength and will give you sound wisdom. *"A friend loves at all times and a brother is born for a time of adversity"* (Proverbs 17:17).
- **Force yourself to laugh.** The Bible teaches that laughter works like good medicine. *"A joyful heart is good medicine, but a crushed spirit dries up the bones"*

3

(Proverbs 17:22). Even when things are at their darkest and most bleak, laughter can ease the pain.

- **Determine to win.** No matter how adverse things may appear, you must keep the attitude that you are going to come out on top. Losing is not an option, nor must it be a part of your vocabulary. Don't let adversity take you out.

When facing adversity, it is important to do what I call "keeping it in a cage." By this, I mean don't let the adversity become all-encompassing. Don't let it consume every area of your life. Keep it confined. If it is a work-related issue, don't take it home with you. Many leaders make the mistake of letting company issues take total control of every area of their lives and negatively affect other things such as spending time with their families. By keeping the adversity compartmentalized, it is easier to focus on solutions to situations while maintaining peace in other areas of your life.

Adversity is a time of growth for a leader. A leader learns lessons in times of adversity that he would not have learned otherwise. This is one of the positive benefits of adversity. Many successful leaders often credit an earlier adverse situation as the reason for their success. It's during adversity that a leader learns who he is and what he is made of. Without adversity there could be no greatness. When athletes win championships, they often talk about the adversity they faced and had to overcome on the way to becoming a champion.

Adversity in leadership cannot be avoided; it is not a matter of if, but rather when and how often it will occur. It will help you or harm you. It will make you or break you. It will either be your gold mine or your graveyard. Leaders should brace themselves for adversity and the pressure that comes with it. How should leaders respond to adversity? They should respond by letting it shape their character and fuel their greatness.

2

Attitude

"If you think you can, you can. And if you think you can't, you're right."

—Mary Kay Ash

"Men are not prisoners of fate, but only prisoners of their own minds."

—Franklin D. Roosevelt

"I can't change the direction of the wind, but I can adjust my sails to always reach my destination."

—Jimmy Dean

"Attitude is a little thing that makes a big difference."

—Winston Churchill

Attitude is a powerful force in the life of a leader. It will either be the leader's best friend or worst enemy. There are basically two types of attitudes: a positive and a negative attitude. A positive attitude is a leader's best friend, while a negative attitude is a leader's worst enemy. A leader with a positive attitude is optimistic, meaning that he chooses to anticipate the best possible outcome to any situation. He sees sunshine on rainy days, the breaking of day in dark times, the glass half full instead of half empty, he smiles when the circumstances say frown, and he laughs when the situation says cry. A positive attitude is priceless. It is more valuable to a leader than silver and gold. You cannot purchase a positive attitude...either you have it or you don't. You can, however, develop one; it is a matter of choice.

You must protect your positive attitude by disconnecting from negative influences. You will never develop a positive attitude hanging around negative people. There must be a cutting of the cord. You have to be around people with positive attitudes to receive the impartation of a positive attitude. This is a critical decision for a leader.

A leader with a negative attitude, on the other hand, is always pessimistic; he chooses to see the worst in everything and every situation. A negative attitude hovers over a leader like a dark cloud and renders him ineffective. A sure way for a leader to commit self-sabotage and leadership suicide is to maintain a negative attitude that goes unchecked and unchanged.

The powerful thing about attitude is that it is a choice, your choice. No one can choose your attitude for you but you. God's sovereignty has placed that decision in your hands and yours alone. As a leader, one cannot blame his peers, his followers or anyone else for that matter, for his imprudent attitude. The only way to keep a good and positive attitude is to decide that you will not let the things that happen to you, determine how you feel within.

Every leader will be challenged in the attitude zone. Leading people is not easy, and many times, those who you are leading contribute greatly to making your job even more difficult. However, you must guard your attitude like a knight guards the royal palace. The moment you allow your attitude to go negative, you have begun the downward spiral of losing your leadership effectiveness.

It has been said that your attitude determines your altitude. Leaders who maintain a positive attitude always achieve and thrive. Determine how high you want to go and adjust your attitude to that height. Some of the benefits of a good attitude are:

- **Achieving success**. Without a positive attitude, achieving success or meeting a goal is almost impossible.
- **Greatly motivated**. A good attitude gives a leader greater energy and motivation; this inspires others.
- **Overcoming obstacles**. Leaders with good attitudes smile at obstacles. They see them as opportunities to successfully climb insurmountable walls.
- **Conquering life**. Life does not give you what you deserve, but what you demand.
- **Winning respect**. People sympathize with losers, but they respect winners and all winners possess a great positive attitude.

John Maxwell gives a powerful assessment of what an attitude is in his book *The Winning Attitude*. Concerning our attitude, he states:

It is the "advance man" of our true selves.

Its roots are inward, but its fruits are outward.
It is our best friend or worst enemy.
It is more honest and more consistent than our
words.
It is an outward look based on past experiences.
It is a thing which draws people to us or repels
them.
It is never content until it is expressed.
It is the librarian of our past.
It is the speaker of our present.
It is the prophet of our future.[1]

The leader's attitude will affect the entire organization. It will determine whether the environment is pleasant, warm and inviting, or if it is unpleasant, tense, cold and uninviting. Though you cannot control all the things that happen in the organization or how the people will act, the one thing you are in total control of is your attitude. Lou Holtz, the famous football coach said, "Life is ten percent of what happens to you and ninety percent how you respond to it." As long as your attitude is positive, any problem or situation is conquerable. Keep a positive attitude.

3

Balance

"At times, it is difficult to keep a proper balance in our lives. But, over time, an improper balance will lead to problems."

—Catherine Pulsifer

"I've learned that you can't have everything and do everything at the same time."

—Oprah Winfrey

"The challenge of work-life balance is without question one of the most significant struggles faced by modern man"

—Steven Covey

"Balance is not better time management, but better boundary management. Balance means making choices and enjoying those choices."

—Betsy Jacobson

Balance is the stability produced by an even distribution of weight on each side of the vertical axis. It simply means that whatever the vertical axis is, you split it down the middle. You stand with one foot on each side. As it regards leadership, balance is essential, but many times overlooked. One of the greatest challenges that a leader will face is the quest to find balance.

The difficulty of this is that there are so many areas of leadership in which the leader must find balance. This also includes the leader's private life. In leadership, the leader must balance showing sensitivity and exerting authority, as well as demonstrating a loose versus tight leadership style. Leaders have to understand the balance of leading change while preserving certain parts of the organizational culture. They must balance policies and procedures with organizational priorities. They must lead change and progress while balancing leadership strategies to manage the change. They must balance autocratic and democratic leadership. An active leader makes things happen, orchestrates change and makes decisions unilaterally and individually. A passive leader delegates tasks to others, allows change to happen naturally and engages in participative, shared decision making.

Finding this balance is key to successful leadership. In their private lives, leaders must find balance between their leadership responsibilities and their personal responsibilities. Personal responsibilities involve things such as being a spouse, being a parent, spending time with the family, going to little league ball games, dance recitals, PTA meetings, etc. It is imperative that leaders find this balance because if they don't, the imbalance will manifest itself in some very ugly ways and at very inopportune times.

The lack of balance leads to the lack of effectiveness. The road of imbalance has led many leaders to become private failures in their personal lives, while appearing to be public successes in their professional lives. The truth is that while imbalance in a leader's life may be personal, it is never private. A leader's visibility makes it inevitable that private failures will be displayed publicly. For this reason, it behooves every leader to find the proper balances in their life whereas not to sabotage their leadership. Some steps to finding balance are as follows:

- **Establish your priorities**. You will never find balance until you establish your priorities. Priorities are imperative because they force you to say yes to the things that are important and no to the things that are not.
- **Get your life in order**. This is getting organized and getting all the clutter out. High performers are orderly and they schedule their days, weeks, months, and years. The result is that they get more out of life.
- **Be flexible**. You must adapt to changes in your routine. Life or business does not always go by the script we have written. If you are inflexible, changes will throw you out of balance.
- **Avoid complication**. Most things in life are simple until we complicate them. Look for the simplest route in every situation. Many great problems have been solved with simple solutions. Follow the old saying, "Keep it simple."
- **Make yourself accountable.** Bring a friend or two along on this process who will hold you accountable for finding balance in your life. Have weekly checkups with your accountability partners. Give them permission to

speak truthfully to you and enforce the rules you have established.

- **Eliminate time wasters.** Take an honest look at how you are spending your time and eliminate the nonessential things pulling at your time. These can range from things that can be delegated to others or people that just need to be purged from your life. This can be a difficult process, but it is extremely necessary.
- **Play as you work.** A healthy life revolves around three things: work, play and rest. Most leaders work very hard but play very little. You must find time for personal enjoyment away from the work load. It is beneficial for your mental and physical health to have fun activities in your life.

The struggle to find balance is a never ending battle that a leader is constantly fighting. To win means that the leader has merged in perfect harmony their professional and personal lives. They have successfully distributed their public and private lives equally on each side of the vertical axis. Balance is about how you live your life and manage your business and people. Paul Boese described balance the best when he said, "We come into this world head first and go out feet first, in between, is all a matter of balance."

4

Belief

"They conquer who believe they can."

—John Dryden

"Mix a conviction with a man and something happens."

—Adam Clayton Powell Jr.

"To accomplish great things, we must not only act, but also dream; not only plan, but also believe."

—Anatole France

"The thing always happens that you really believe in; and the belief in a thing makes it happen."

—Frank Lloyd Wright

Belief is the inner conviction deep down on the inside of leaders that tells them they can accomplish the seemingly impossible, conquer the seemingly unconquerable, and win in the face of insurmountable odds. Belief is what keeps a leader's dreams alive. The course of a leader's life is charted by the dream in the leader's heart. If the leader stops believing and allows the dream to die, there is nothing to chart his life by. At this point, the leader is like an abandoned boat on rough seas, going in whatever direction the wind blows and the waves carry it.

Belief is the faith that tells the leader that victory is inevitable. In the times when conflict, turmoil, and tension cause doubt to arise (regarding whether the organization will prevail, or if his leadership stand), the followers look to the leader to find faith and a ray of hope. They want to know if the leader still believes. A leader must be so full of belief and faith in his vision, purpose, and calling that it infects everyone around him so they, too, believe they are invincible. Nothing is impossible to a leader who is full of belief, and nothing can stop a leader who refuses to doubt and be denied victory.

Belief is a leader's best friend in times of great adversity. So, whatever you do as a leader, don't stop believing. A leader who is strong in the area of belief will see an obstacle as a challenge, and opposition as an opportunity. A leader's belief will be challenged at every stage of his growth, at every level of advancement, and at every attempt to accomplish a great feat.

A study of great leaders, both historical and contemporary, will show they all possessed that strong belief or inner conviction in themselves and what they were called to do—that is what thrust them into greatness. Nelson Mandela is a perfect example of this. His belief in freedom for his people caused him to revolt against the oppressive system of apartheid. He spent twenty-seven years in prison for his convictions, and his belief that his people would be free never wavered.

His revolution would transform a model of racial division and oppression into an open democracy that would elect him president. Of himself, Mandela says, "I was not a messiah, but an ordinary man who had become a leader because of extraordinary circumstances." Like Mandela, a leader should not only possess belief, but belief should possess the leader. Leaders who are consumed with belief are unstoppable, unbeatable, and undeterred in their quest to obtain their objectives and goals. They are the movers and shakers, they are change agents, they are the ones who shape history, become legends, and whose names are never forgotten. There are several things that a leader must believe in, they are:

- **Himself.** You must believe in your God-given abilities and talents. No one else will believe in you if you don't believe in yourself, and you won't get very far if you don't believe in yourself. As the leader, you must display confidence and belief in the organization at all times.
- **The Team**. You must believe in the team helping you win, and the team must know that you believe in them. This will bring the best out of them. Something happens to a team in a very positive way when they know that the leader believes in them no matter what. They rise up and perform at a higher level than the norm.
- **Mentors.** You must believe in the people who are developing you as a leader. You must be willing to follow their advice even when you don't understand it, because you trust their wisdom and experience. You must believe they know what they are doing, where they are taking you and that they have your best interest at heart.

- **The Vision**. You must believe in the vision you are pursuing and the strategy to get you there. Belief in the vision is your fuel for the journey, and it is what will carry you through rough terrain and dark times. It is your belief in the vision that says, "We will prevail, we will win."

Henry Ford once said, "Whether you believe you can do a thing or not, you are right." Belief works both ways, it works for you if you believe you can and it works against you if you believe you can't. The Bible has a very powerful declaration about belief in Mark 9:23, *And Jesus said to him, "'If You can?' All things are possible to him who believes."* Effective leaders always believe they can and they believe they will, and because of their belief they always do.

5

Comfort Zone

"Only those who dare to fail greatly can ever achieve greatly.

—Robert F. Kennedy

"Don't be afraid to go out on a limb. That's where the fruit is."

—Arthur F. Lenehan

"If you remain in your comfort zone you will not go any further."

—Catherine Pulsifer

"Life loses its meaning when we get stuck up in comfort zone."

—M. K. Soni

A comfort zone denotes the limited set of behaviors and environments that a person can engage in without becoming nervous. A comfort zone is the abode of leaders who think small. They live and die in their comfort zones because they fear leaving the boundaries they have established for themselves. Small thinking leaders never leave their place of comfort; therefore, they never accomplish anything of significance.

There are two reasons that leaders are afraid to leave their comfort zones. First, they are afraid of failure, and second, they are afraid of rejection. Small thinking leaders are paralyzed by these two fears. Leaders who think large understand that in order to go to higher levels of greatness and accomplishment, they must constantly break out of their comfort zones. They have conquered and trampled underfoot the fear of failure and rejection.

There are two things that are common about the comfort zones of leaders who think large. First, their comfort zones are always changing, and second, they are only in them temporarily. They are always changing because the place at one point that was considered out of their comfort zone becomes a comfort zone as they progress toward their goal or destiny. The reason they are always in them temporarily is that they don't allow themselves to get comfortable and satisfied in one place or with one accomplishment. They are constantly leaving their comfort zones because they recognize that the next challenge is over the horizon beyond their comfort zone. Once out of their comfort zone, they embrace the new territory and soon become comfortable with it. The new territory soon becomes a new comfort zone.

Great leaders are always creating new comfort zones. They are driven by challenges. When they slay one giant, rather than settle in and get comfortable with that victory, they seek other giants to slay. When they climb one mountain, they look for the next mountain to conquer. Their inner drive will not let them get comfortable. Their quest for greatness and significance is always calling them out of their comfort zone.

Comfort zones can become to a leader what prison walls are to an inmate. After being in prison for an extended period, the convict gets so adjusted to life behind the prison walls that upon his release from prison, he cannot function in society as a normal citizen. In prison life, this is called institutionalization. A leader can become so accustomed to his comfort zone that he becomes institutionalized by it. When this happens, the leader has plateaued in his growth and his leadership begins a downward track instead of maintaining a steady climb.

Although breaking out of a comfort zone is not easy, it is necessary for the leader to press through the pain and fears to break free. How does a leader break out of the comfort zone?

- **Face your fears**. Franklin D. Roosevelt said, "You have nothing to fear but fear itself." Fear is the reason leaders are trapped in a comfort zone. You have to make a firm decision to face and conquer your fears. If you don't, your fears will paralyze you as a leader and exterminate every seed of greatness in you. Don't let fear rob and hold you back another day.
- **Take small steps**. You don't have to do it all at once. The journey of a thousand miles starts with the first step. Decide what your first step should be. If you fall on that first step, get back up and try it again. Failure is not falling down, it's refusing to get up.
- **Try something new**. Nothing breaks us out of old habits like trying something new. Some years back, I started playing golf which was light years out of my comfort

zone. I was very nervous, at first, just to step onto the course because I felt intimidated. Now I feel at home on any course in America because I faced and conquered my fears. Golf has opened up a whole new world to me.
• **Stick to it.** Once you get out of your comfort zone, do not go back, no matter how strange it feels. You will become familiar to the new surroundings in short order. The more I played golf, the more comfortable I felt in that environment. Resolute tenacity or persistence will cause you to overcome and thrive in the new comfort zone.

Breaking out of one's comfort zone is the only pathway to greatness. It is the only road to a lasting legacy. It is a road that only the courageous dare to travel. Is there fear along this road? Yes, but the upside is greater than the downside. The freedom to soar and the rewards gained provide the fortitude necessary for a leader to break out of the institutionalization of a comfort zone. Because leaders understand this is the only path to greatness, they hear the call to greatness and they respond to it.

6

Commitment

"Commitment unlocks the doors of imagination, allows vision, and gives us the right stuff to turn our dreams into reality."

—James Womack

"I can't imagine a person becoming a success who doesn't give this game of life everything he's got."

—Walter Cronkite

"It was character that got us out of bed, commitment that moved us into action and discipline that enabled us to follow through."

—Zig Ziglar

"Commitment is the enemy of resistance, for it is the serious promise to press on, to get up, no matter how many times you are knocked down."

—David McNally

Commitment is the driving force behind high impact leaders. They don't have to search for commitment because it is one of those intangibles that they naturally possess. Commitment is not only the single most important factor to success, but it is also one of the non-negotiables of great leadership. Commitment is what causes great leaders to reach the top of their game, and it is what causes them to stay at the top of their game.

The commitment of great leaders is not determined nor deterred by their feelings, their emotions, or by their circumstances. Their commitment is determined by an unquenchable desire to succeed and win at the highest level. These types of leaders are driven with an obsession to succeed and accomplish great exploits. One of the common characteristics of all great leaders throughout history and contemporary times is a very high level of commitment. Some examples of committed leaders are:

- **Alexander the Great**. He was committed to world conquest. He accomplished this by age 32. Legend has it that when Alexander saw the breath of his domain, he wept for there were no more worlds to conquer.
- **Julius Caesar**. He was committed to expanding the Roman Empire and reforming the Roman government. He is historically recognized as one of the greatest military and political leaders of all time.
- **Apostle Paul**. He was committed to spreading the gospel to the Gentiles. He is considered the greatest of the apostles. He wrote half of the New Testament. His commitment to Christ ultimately cost him his life.
- **George Washington**. He was committed to leading the American Revolution to bring freedom to this new

country. He was the first president and a true visionary whose vision still endures today.

- **Abraham Lincoln**. He was committed to ending the travesty of slavery. He is credited with ending slavery in the United States by signing the Emancipation Proclamation. He was a determined leader with an enormous amount of courage in some very turbulent times. His commitment to ending slavery brought about his assassination.

- **Martin Luther King, Jr.** He was committed to obtaining equality for his people. He was thrust into the leadership of a movement that touched the soul of America and forced upon this nation the fair treatment for people of color. He is known as the dreamer because he had a dream of what this country should be like. Because of his commitment, he was killed by an assassin's bullet. However, his dream still lives on.

These are only a few examples of committed leaders, but we see in them a commitment to their cause in spite of the price they had to pay. Followers feed off the commitment of the leader. Michael Jordan was arguably the greatest player to ever play the game of basketball. His talent was unmatched. However, what most people do not know is that Michael was also one of the most committed players to ever play the game. It is said that Michael played harder in practice than he did in the game and that the Bulls' practices were more intense than the games. Michael was the first player to arrive at practice and the last one to leave.

The rest of the Bulls' players picked up and fed off Michael's commitment, resulting in the Bulls having one of the greatest dynasties in NBA history. They had six championships in the

1990's. Their dynasty was not stopped by another team, but rather by a general manager who broke up the team because he was more committed to his own ego and agenda than to allowing history to continue.

Commitment for a leader does not begin when he finally takes the mantle of leadership. It begins long before he ever becomes a leader (during the time when he is insignificant in the organization). It is his commitment outside the spotlight (when there are no accolades), that propels him to leadership. The sports teams who win championships don't win the championship on the championship game day. They win it back in training camp when there are no cameras or reporters; that is the place where the commitment to do what is necessary to be a champion is made. The same is true with leaders, the commitment is made outside the grand stage. A leader must be committed to several things:

- **His Assignment**. If he fails here, nothing else matters. People won't follow a leader who is not committed to his assignment or his calling. People don't mind getting into the fray with the leader as long as they see his unwavering commitment.
- **His Team**. A breakdown here makes lasting success virtually impossible. The people have to know that the leader is highly committed to them before they make a deep-rooted commitment to the leader.
- **Continued Growth**. If the leader stops growing, so does the organization. The leader must be committed to developing a growth environment within the organization. He must lead by example because his commitment to growth becomes contagious.

- **Constant Improvement**. He is always seeking ways to improve the organization. He must ask the question, "How do we get better?" His commitment here will prevent the spirit of complacency from infiltrating the organization.
- **Ethics**. The effectiveness of a leader depends upon his ethical principles. The leader must not only be committed to doing the right things, but he must also be committed to doing the right things the right way. When the leader is committed to the highest ethical standards, he can demand the same standards from the followers.
- **Integrity**. There is nothing worse than a leader who has no integrity. A leader's reputation is determined by his commitment, or lack thereof, to a life of integrity. It doesn't matter how gifted or talented a leader may be—a lack of integrity will sabotage his leadership. *"A good name is to be more desired than great wealth..."* (Proverbs 22:1).

A lack of commitment to a leader is like kryptonite to Superman. It weakens his leadership and eventually kills it. No leader can last very long in the game of leadership without commitment. Commitment is one of those intangibles that you cannot teach a leader, he either has it or he doesn't have it. When commitment exists, you can see it in the leader's eyes, actions, and in everything he says and does. It is a thing of beauty to study and observe a committed leader.

7

Decisions

"Decision is a sharp knife that cuts clean and straight; indecision, a dull one that hacks and tears and leaves ragged edges behind it."
—Gordon Graham

"We know what happens to people who stay in the middle of the road. They get run over."
—Aneurin Bevan

"Nothing is more difficult, and therefore more precious, than to be able to decide."
—Napoleon Bonaparte

"You can't make decisions based on fear and the possibility of what might happen."
— Michelle Obama

Leadership is all about making decisions. The greater the level of leadership, the greater the leader's responsibilities are and the decisions he must make. The decisions that a leader makes are of the utmost importance because a leader's decisions affect other people and the organization as a whole. A bad decision on the part of a leader can spell disaster and have repercussions that may take years in which to recover.

Decisions mark the measure of the leader. Good leaders are good because they make good decisions; poor leaders are poor because they have made poor decisions. In his book *Good to Great*, Jim Collins refers to the leaders who have taken their companies from being good to great as Level 5 leaders. He identifies their ability to make good, hard, and risky decisions. Collins says, "Level 5 leaders are resolved to do whatever it takes to make the company great, no matter how big or hard the decisions."[2]

Leadership demands leaders who can see quickly and act instantaneously. Leaders cannot afford the luxury of indecision and hesitation. Leaders are sometimes required to act while the picture is still a bit cloudy. An example of this is the killing of Osama bin Laden. During his campaign for the presidency, President Obama said that if he had Osama bin Laden in sight, he would give the order to kill him. In August of 2010, intelligence came to President Obama that there was a high probability that Osama bin Laden was in a compound in Abbottabad, Pakistan. After several months of surveillance, there still was not one hundred percent certainty he was there. President Obama had to make a decision whether or not to raid the compound. If he ordered the raid and Osama bin Laden was not there, it would severely damage his presidency and cripple his chances for re-election. The picture was not crystal clear, cloudy to say the least, nevertheless, he made the decision to go in, and on May

2, 2011, the Navy Seals raided the compound and killed Osama bin Laden. It was a risky decision, but it was the right decision made with a cloudy picture.

If a leader waits to measure every difficulty and balance every perplexity he faces, he will do very little. Hesitant leadership is weak leadership. In some instances, it is more excusable for a leader to make a wrong decision than to be in a continually wavering position. A decision delayed by a leader until it is too late is not a decision, it is an evasion. Decisions are at the heart of a leader's success.

There are times when the decisions that a leader must make are difficult and critical to the organization or people he is leading. Making decisions is an enormous responsibility that is placed upon a leader. A person who is afraid or doesn't want to make decisions should never occupy a leadership position. While there is no great secret to making decisions, there are steps that can be followed that will be helpful in making decisions. They are as follows:

- **Define the decision**. What is the decision that must be made? A leader can't make a decision until he knows what decision must be made.
- **Clarify your objectives**. What am I trying to accomplish? This gives the leader the clarity needed to make a right decision.
- **Prioritize your objectives**. What are the non-negotiables? These are the things that are firmly established and are not open to discussion, modification, or compromise.
- **Identify the alternatives**. What is Plan B? Leaders would be wise to have an alternative. It is there only as a just in case.

- **Evaluate the alternatives**. Is Plan B a viable choice? It should be almost as good as the original plan in that it might have to be used.
- **Assess the risk**. What are the consequences? There are no decisions without consequences. A leader has to be willing to live with the consequences of his decisions.
- **Make a decision**. After gathering all the facts and answering all the questions, there is no need for any further delay, pull the trigger.

Good decision making requires that a leader be of sound mind and emotionally stable. The leader has to be able to control his impulses so that he will not be lured into making emotional or irrational decisions that create permanent consequences in what might otherwise be a temporary situation. When a leader allows emotions to drive decisions, it is equivalent to driving an automobile down the highway blindfolded. A leader has to take responsibility for the decisions he makes, as well as having a full comprehension of the consequences of the decision being made. In other words, the leader must make sure beyond any doubt that he can stand the consequences before the decision is made.

A leader cannot avoid the decision-making process. Welcome the fact that all of your decisions are not going to be popular or well received. Criticizing and second-guessing of your decisions by others comes with the territory, so don't be moved by it and do not take it personally. In other words, a leader cannot be thin-skinned.

Leaders must make sure that their decisions will yield the desired results. They should never go to war where there are no spoils. If there is nothing to be gained, don't fight. Choose your battles wisely. Make sure that what you are fighting for is worth the price you will pay. These decisions cannot be delegated. The leader has to make them. This is why he is the leader, to make the tough decisions.

8

Discipline

"No man is fit to command another that cannot command himself."

—William Penn

"Discipline is the bridge between goals and accomplishments."

—Jim Rohn

"Nothing is more harmful to service than the neglect of discipline; for that discipline, more than numbers, gives one Army superiority over another."

—George Washington

"Discipline yourself, and others won't need to."

—John Wooden

Discipline can be defined as the training needed to produce a specific character or pattern of behavior, especially training that produces moral, physical, or mental development in a particular direction. Discipline is absolutely necessary for a leader to succeed and perform at maximum potential. A leader without discipline is like an automobile without gas. It has the potential for forward movement, but it lacks the necessary fuel. Discipline is what keeps a leader on course and focused on his vision, goals and objectives.

When you study the habits of highly successful and effective leaders, you will find that there are certain disciplines that are maintained. They are committed to their disciplines with a religious like commitment. These are the great leaders. In contrast, poor leaders lack the necessary discipline to cause them to be more effective. The discipline of great leaders causes them to be proactive, whereas the lack of discipline of poor leaders causes them to be reactive. Discipline involves being able to do the same things over and over for an extended period of time until it becomes a part of you. It becomes second nature.

In athletics, athletes are so drilled in certain disciplines that they can wake up in the wee hours of the morning and do the drill while half asleep. This is the same discipline that is required to be a great leader. Great leaders are so schooled and disciplined on the art and principles of leadership, that they view everything and make every decision from a leadership perspective.

The lack of discipline in a leader will lead to disaster in the organization. The lack of discipline is probably the most common cause of failure in the life of a leader. I call this lack of discipline, cheating. I once heard Muhammad Ali discuss training for one of his three epic fights with Joe Frazier. He spoke of the cold mornings getting up at 4:00 a.m. to run the back roads of those Pennsylvania Mountains. The temperatures would sometimes be well below freezing, and the swirling winds made it almost unbearable. He said that there were plenty of days he did not want to get up and face the cold temperatures to run those five to ten miles, and he thought of cheating by not running or by doing one or two miles instead of five or ten. When pressed to cheat, he came to the realization that if he cheated on those cold mornings, when he got into the ring with Frazier and the fight progressed, Frazier would know by his lack of stamina that he cheated during his training back at Deer Lake, Pennsylvania. Not only would Frazier know that he cheated, but the world would know that he cheated. It was that realization that caused him to stay true to the discipline of training that thrust him to victory and made him the champion he was.

Many leaders have cheated, and in some cases, everyone knows it. The lack of discipline and cheating may be personal, but it is never private. There will come a time when everyone will see very clearly that you cheated in your training. Discipline is not easy, in fact, it's painful and challenging, nonetheless, the rewards are most fulfilling. Every leader must look in the mirror and face himself and ask the question, "Is the reward worth the discipline?" When you look at the discipline the truly great leaders have developed in their lives and the commitment they make to maintain that discipline, you see what gives them the edge and what separates them from average leaders. The average leader wants the edge that the great ones have, but they are unwilling to pay the necessary price. They don't understand that great leadership doesn't come at bargain basement prices. There are several areas in a leader's life wherein he must maintain discipline:

- **Vision**. Discipline here allows the leader to say yes to some things and no to others. This keeps the leader from being all over the place and into everything.

- **Goals**. Discipline here allows the leader to always keep his goals in view, no matter what the circumstances. This keeps the leader determined and undeterred.
- **Focus**. Discipline here allows the leader to keep the main thing, the main thing. This keeps everything in the proper perspective for the leader.
- **Time**. Discipline here allows the leader to maximize each 24-hour period. This keeps the leader managing his time.
- **Growth**. Discipline here keeps the leader in a lifelong learning posture. This keeps the leader from plateauing and stagnation.

Jim Rohn says, "There are two types of pain you will go through in life, the pain of discipline and the pain of regret. Discipline weighs ounces while regret weighs tons." That quote resonates true as it relates to leaders also. The leaders who pay the price and pain of discipline reap rewards for their work. In the end they discover that the gains were worth the price. However, leaders who don't pay the price of discipline carry a burden of regret that unceasingly plagues them. They preferred convenience over discipline and their reward was a harvest of regret.

During an interview, the head of an organization was asked if he regretted all the things that he had to sacrifice and walk away from to build his company into a dominant force in their industry. His reply was, "That's the discipline, no regrets." A leader who thrives to be a serious mover and shaker must come to a place of resolve where he looks at the price for greatness and without the slightest bit of hesitation says, "That's the discipline."

9

Ethics

"I would prefer even to fail with honor than win by cheating."

—**Sophocles**

"Right is right, even if everyone is against it; and wrong is wrong, even if everyone is for it."

—**William Penn**

"Ask yourself not if this or that is expedient, but if it is right."

—**Alan Paton**

"A man without ethics is a wild beast loosed upon this world."

—**Albert Camus**

Ethics has several different definitions. However, when applied to leaders and leadership, the best way to define ethics is a set of moral principles or values which determine the rules and standards of conduct. Within the professional arena, ethics are a set of professional standards containing aspects of fairness and duty to the profession and the general public. Ayn Rand once stated that, "Ethics is a code of values which guide our choices and actions and determines the purpose and course of our lives."

Ethics is an important aspect to a leader because one's ethical behavior can define a person's capacity for leadership. Ethics refers to the study and development of one's ethical standards. It behooves every leader to constantly examine his standards to ensure that they are sensible and logical. Ethics also means, then, the continuous effort of studying our own moral beliefs and moral conduct, and striving to ensure that we, and the organizations we lead, live up to standards that are rational and solid.

People look to leaders for motivation, guidance, and role modeling. If there are questions concerning a leader's ethics, the leader's ability to effectively motivate, guide, and be a role model are compromised. When a person becomes the leader of an organization, he is given a goodwill account. John Maxwell calls this, "change in his pocket." During his tenure as leader, he builds up that account if he does well for the company. Some leaders have built up plenty of goodwill in their accounts. They have a lot of change in their pockets. However, ethical mishaps can cost a leader a great deal of goodwill. With every misstep, he has to reach in his pocket and give up some of that change. Eventually, he will run out of change if he continues to have missteps. His goodwill account will be labeled "non-sufficient funds."

Every leader will face opportunities to do things that are unethical in one area or another. There will be opportunities that others may never know about. Sometimes, it is not even a matter of law as much as it is a matter of conscience. A person of ethics does not gauge the matter upon who will and who will not know, but rather by his own self and conscience which he will face every time he looks into the mirror. The following is an acronym for ethics:

- **Expectations**. Leaders are expected to have high ethical standards. *"For unto whosoever much is given, of him shall much be required"* (Luke 12:48).
- **Trust**. Where trust is broken, the influence of leadership collapses. Trust is the foundation of leadership. Everything a leader does is built on trust.
- **Honor**. Ethics, or the lack thereof, will bring a leader honor or dishonor. General Colin Powell is an example of honor bestowed upon a leader with high ethics. General David Petraeus is an example of the dishonor that comes when a leader has ethical missteps.
- **Integrity**. This is one of the cornerstones of leadership. When this is gone, there is nothing left. The road to restoring integrity is a long, uphill climb.
- **Code.** Every leader must live and function by a set of moral codes. A leader without a moral code is like fallen leaves on a windy day; they go where the wind blows.
- **Standard**. When it comes to high ethical standards, the leader is the straw that stirs the drink. The leader sets the standard and others follow it.

Golf is a game of ethics. It is a game in which there are no referees or umpires; therefore, every player polices himself. In the movie, *The Legend of Bagger Vance*, one of the competing golfers, Rannulph Junah (played by Matt Damon), in a very important match, had his ball in a small rough. The ball came to rest upon a small stick. When Junah moved the stick, the ball moved about an inch, which is a violation of the rules and results in a one stroke penalty. The match was close and for Junah to report the penalty would surely cost him the match. No one saw the ball move but Junah and a little boy, Hardy Greaves (played by J. Michael Moncrief), who was helping to caddy for him. With tears streaming down his face, Greaves pleaded with Junah not to report it because no one saw it. "No one will know," Greaves pleaded with Junah. Junah replied, "I will know." Then he proceeded to call his opponents and the marshal over to report what had happened. It ended up costing him a chance to win the match. (Bobby Jones actually did this during the 1925 U.S. Open and would later go on to lose by one stroke).[3]

Junah's decision is an example of the essence of ethics, when no one would have known, he was still honest. Every time he looked in the mirror, he would have known that he cheated. As leaders, we are constantly being honored for achievements and with that honor comes hurrahs and applause. The real question to a leader is would the people still be hurrahing and applauding if they knew what we know about all of our ethics? Have we moved the ball and said nothing? Did we take credit for an achievement that was flawed because we cheated a little bit? Every leader must answer these questions for himself. He must face the man in the mirror. Sometimes, a leader has to stand alone on the side of ethics.

Society dictates the norms of the culture and of the times. There are occasions when the norms in society are in direct contrast to the ethical positions that a leader has developed. Some leaders flip flop on ethical positions due to the pressure put upon them by different segments of society. However, it is at times like this that the true character of a leader is shown. He makes the decision to stand by his convictions and to stand alone if necessary. It is in that hour that a leader says, "I have to live with myself; I will see that I have good company."

10

Excellence

"Excellence is doing ordinary things extraordinarily well."

—John W. Gardner

"It is a wretched taste to be gratified with mediocrity when the excellent lies before us."

—Isaac Disraeli

"Perfection is our goal, excellence will be tolerated."

—J. Yahl

"Perfection is not attainable, but if we chase perfection we can catch excellence."

—Vince Lombardi

Throughout history, the word excellence has been used as a title of honor. It is derived from the word excel which means to surpass. Every leader should strive for excellence in everything he does relative to his leadership. In the early 1990's, when the Lexus automobile was first introduced, Lexus had a slogan regarding how they approached manufacturing their cars that said, "The relentless pursuit of perfection." As leaders, we may never reach perfection, but we should have an attitude of a relentless pursuit of excellence.

Excellence should be the goal of every leader regardless of the arena in which he leads. Furthermore, J. Hampton Keathley, III defines the pursuit of excellence for it is "not to be a quest for superiority," and is not about "competition" or about "outstripping others," which is "usually done for one's own glory or significance or for the praise or applause of men." Instead, he quotes Harbour distinguishing between success and excellence, saying that "Success means being the best. Excellence means being your best. Success, to many, means being better than everyone else. Excellence means being better tomorrow than you were yesterday. Success means exceeding the achievements of other people. Excellence means matching your practice with your potential."[4]

Leaders should never become comfortable or satisfied with average and mediocrity. As Isaac D' Israeli once said, "It is a wretched taste to be gratified with mediocrity when the excellent lies before us." In a leader's heart, there must be a commitment to excellence. Excellence is not a skill but rather an attitude. It is the attitude to push one's self to be the very best that you can be at whatever you do or doing the very best job on any given task. Excellence, in other words, can be summed up as maximizing one's potential or to function at the highest possible level. It is this attitude that makes the great ones great, and it is what makes champions become champions. When leaders pass on the pursuit of excellence, they become ordinary and quickly plateau in their development as a leader. The quest for excellence keeps us ever growing and thriving for the next level. The pursuit of excellence is the fuel and energy that gives us lift off from the launching pad of average and mediocrity and allows us to soar into the regions of untapped potential and possibility. It keeps us from drifting along on the sea of limited productivity and achievement. Excellence is not perfection and we should not lump them together. Perfection means that we are flawless. That distinction belongs to God and God alone. Excellence means that I strive to be better than I already am. It means that I am in a constant state of improvement. John Maxwell lays out eleven keys to achieving excellence in his leadership lesson, *Eleven Keys To Excellence.* I will list several of his keys to which I have added a quote.

- **Don't Settle for Average**. *"The difference between an Olympic gold medalist and a silver medalist in the 100 meter race is 1/10 of a second and millions of dollars."* (P. Ronald Wilder)
- **Pay Attention to Details**. *"Beware of the small expenses; a small leak will sink a great ship."* (Benjamin Franklin)
- **Develop a Deep Commitment to Excellence**. *"First we will be the best, then we will be first."* (Stan Leonard)
- **Be Consistent**. *"Just as sure as the sun is to come up every morning, so must you be in your pursuit of excellence."* (P. Ronald Wilder)
- **Never Stop Improving**. *"The quest for excellence is striving to get better every single day of your life."* (P. Ronald Wilder)

- **Make Excellence a Lifestyle.** *"You don't pay for excellence and success on an installment plan, you pay up front."* (P. Ronald Wilder)

Excellence involves continuous improvement. This improvement and the pursuit of excellence are both challenging and constant. It is challenging because it is not easy and constant because there is no end point. Excellence, is always moving. Once you get to your point of perceived excellence, it (excellence) will have moved to another place—one that is more difficult to reach. However, no matter how difficult it is to achieve the pursuit of excellence, leaders should continue to strive for it.

Excellence does not come without its enemies. Some of the enemies of excellence are:

- **Excuses.** This is the exemption from responsibility. It has been said that excuses are tools of the incompetent used to build monuments of nothingness, and those who specialize in them seldom accomplish anything.
- **Complacency.** This is self-satisfaction without the awareness of deficiencies. Complacency does not require that a leader attempt to get better. Why keep growing? Why strive for excellence? You are content as you are.
- **Fear.** This is the enemy of the leader's faith that he can achieve the goal. Fear will keep the leader on the runway afraid to take off. It will terminate every great thing down inside a leader.
- **Laziness.** This is the refusal to labor and go to the extreme to achieve excellence. Laziness tells the leader that the price for excellence is too great to pay, the hill to excellence is too high to climb and discipline is too demanding.

- **Average.** This is a major enemy of excellence because it is the path most taken. A leader cannot be satisfied with average and pursue excellence at the same time. He must choose one or the other. There is no middle ground.

Achieving and maintaining excellence in leadership is not something that is easy to do. If it were, everyone would do it. The road to excellence is not crowded. There are no traffic jams along the way. The reason for this is that many leaders accept the status quo. This is the path of least resistance. It is not the path that great leaders are looking for. They are not looking for the easy way out or the easiest path. If the path to excellence is demanding and challenging, they rise to the challenge and meet the demand.

Lexus' great pursuit of perfection caused them to produce an automobile line that is consistently rated high on the auto charts for performance and durability. This is the result of Lexus' commitment to excellence. They created an incredible culture that promotes thriving for excellence. Excellence is not achieved by accidental occurrences; it is achieved by intentional actions. Lexus has taught us this. Leaders also need to be intentional in their pursuit of excellence.

11

Failure

"Failure is an event, never a person; an attitude, not an outcome."

—Zig Ziglar

"Being defeated is often a temporary condition. Giving up is what makes it permanent."

—Marilyn vos Savant

"You become strong by defying defeat and by turning loss into gain and failure to success."

—Napoleon

"Failure should be our teacher, not our undertaker. Failure is delay, not defeat. It is a temporary detour, not a dead end. Failure is something we can avoid only by saying nothing, doing nothing, and being nothing."

—Denis Waitley

Failure is a word in which all great leaders are familiar. On their journey to successful leadership, leaders have had to pass through the valley of failure. Failure in general refers to the state or condition of not meeting a desired or intended objective. It may be viewed as the opposite of success.[5] Failure is not falling down; failure is falling down and not getting back up. Most successful leaders will tell you that on their success journey came lessons they learned as they endured failures. It is inevitable that failures will occur in the lives of leaders, therefore, a leader's success will be determined by how he handles failure.

There is no leader who has not failed at something while leading. Successful leaders haven't achieved success solely because they learned to avoid failures. They also learned how to persevere through the defeats. Under no such circumstance are they allowed to quit. They have adopted the "failure is not an option" policy. They may encounter failure or defeat on their way to their ultimate goal. However, they never believe that a single failure or a single defeat is final failure or final defeat. This is where the rubber meets the road in leadership.

When a leader experiences failure, he has to dig deep down within himself to find the resolve to get back up and keep on fighting until the failure has been turned into success. It is here that a leader's character is revealed. You see, failure not only builds character, it reveals it. A leader must not fear failure but rather accept the fact that failure is a possibility. If failure were not a possibility, what glory would there be in victory.

One of the all-time greatest hitters in baseball history is Barry Bonds who played for the San Francisco Giants. He is the all-time home run leader for a season (73) and for a career (762). Every time Bonds came to bat, he faced failure. His goal was to hit a homerun; however, he faced the possibility of striking out.

He didn't sit in the dugout and say, "I'm not going to go to bat because I might strike out." Instead, he accepted the challenge and went to bat time and time again. In order to be a hero, there must also be the possibility of being a goat. (In sports, the person who causes the team to lose the game is called the goat). Leadership is no exception. You will look failure directly in the face and it will stare you down trying to get you to fear and give in to it. Most self-made millionaires have either been bankrupted or gone broke on their way to millionaire status. They experienced a failure but they only allowed it to be temporary. They did not let it become their destiny.

How does a leader bounce back from a failure? We can take some clues from a boxer who has been knocked down. There are four things he does to come back from a knock down. I call them the "knock down rules" and they are as follows:

- **He gets a 10 count**. This allows him time to recover from the initial blow and to get back up to continue fighting to survive the round. When leaders are constantly hit with and knocked down by the blows of the job, they should take their 10 count and get back up and endure the rest of the round.
- **After the round, he goes to his corner**. This allows him to rest for one minute and fully recover from the knock down and prepare for the next round. Leaders should take the short breaks afforded them between the rounds to access the situation and be rejuvenated.
- **His corner men attend to him**. The trainer tells him where he made mistakes in order to allow his opponent to knock him down. He also gives him strategic instructions and makes necessary strategy adjustments. His cut man takes care of any cuts or bruises. A leader

must have a trainer and a cut man in his circle of relationships. *"A friend loves at all times, and a brother is born for adversity."* (Proverbs 17:17)

• **He goes out and fights the next round.** He regroups and gets back into the fight determined to put the knock down behind him and win the fight. A leader must regroup and shake off the knock down and get back into the fight with a relentless determination to come out on top.

Leadership can sometimes be like a boxing match. Whether you are leading a large company, a small organization or maybe you just hold a leadership position of some sort, you will have to take your punches and sometimes you will get knocked down. As a leader, you must never allow failure to have the last word. The issue is not if you will be knocked down, but when you are knocked down. How you respond and what you do after the knock down will be the determining factor between victory and defeat. An appropriate response is to follow the knockdown rules.

Many times, the best success stories begin with failure. Abraham Lincoln served as the 16th president of the United States and is regarded as one of the greatest leaders in U.S. history. He is a perfect model of persistence and overcoming failure. Here is a sketch of Lincoln's road to the White House:

• 1816 – His family was forced out of their home. He had to work to support them.
• 1818 – His mother died.
• 1831 – Failed in business.
• 1832 – Ran for state legislature - lost.
• 1832 – Also lost his job - wanted to go to law school but couldn't get in.

- 1833 – Borrowed some money from a friend to begin a business and by the end of the year he was bankrupt. He spent the next 17 years of his life paying off this debt.
- 1834 – Ran for state legislature again - won.
- 1835 – Was engaged to be married, sweetheart died and his heart was broken.
- 1836 – Had a total nervous breakdown and was in bed for six months.
- 1838 – Sought to become speaker of the state legislature - defeated.
- 1840 – Sought to become elector - defeated.
- 1843 – Ran for Congress - lost.
- 1846 – Ran for Congress again - this time he won - went to Washington and did a good job.
- 1848 – Ran for re-election to Congress - lost.
- 1849 – Sought the job of land officer in his home state - rejected.
- 1854 – Ran for Senate of the United States - lost.
- 1856 – Sought the Vice-Presidential nomination at his party's national convention - got less than 100 votes.
- 1858 – Ran for U.S. Senate again - again he lost.
- 1860 – Elected president of the United States.[6]

How did President Lincoln overcome the failure and disappointment he faced? He lived by a code that every leader should adopt and live by. The code is simply this, "Failure is not the end." When a leader commits himself to this code, nothing will be able to stop him.

12

Fear

"Fear is a darkroom where negatives develop."
—Usman B. Asif

"Courage is not the absence of fear, but rather the judgment that something else is more important than fear."
—Ambrose Redmoon

"If a man harbors any sort of fear, it percolates through all his thinking, damages his personality, makes him landlord to a ghost."
—Lloyd Cassel Douglas

"Do the thing you fear to do and keep on doing it... that is the quickest and surest way ever yet discovered to conquer fear."
—Dale Carnegie

Fear is an unpleasant feeling of perceived risk or danger, real or not. Fear also can be described as a feeling of extreme dislike to some conditions/objects; such as: fear of darkness, fear of ghosts, etc. It is one of the basic emotions.[7] Every leader has his fears and must deal with them in one form or another. An illuminating testament of a leader's potential for success is how he deals with his fears.

Fear is a natural emotion that comes upon each of us when we are in or facing certain situations. Therefore, it is not uncommon for a leader to have certain fears. However, a leader must learn to conquer his fears or his fears will take hold of him and control his every action and ultimately his entire life. The reason that a leader must conquer his fears is because fear is a paralyzer. It renders you motionless and shifts you into neutral. It is the enemy of faith and the assassin of greatness. A leader cannot achieve greatness with fear as his constant companion.

With regard to fear, the leader has a choice regarding how to respond to it. He can cave into it and thus struggle with it, or he can withstand it and overcome it. Either way, the choice is in the hands of the leader and not in the hands of fear. Fear does not choose how you respond to it. Some have said that fear is an acronym for:

False
Evidence
Appearing
Real

What this means is that fear takes the uncorroborated assertion about impending doom, magnifies it, and presents the so-called results as certain failure. A leader must not allow his fears to become his chief counselor. Fear has a way of keeping a leader in a mode of indecisiveness.

Is there ever a time when a leader should listen to the counsel of his fears? If he doesn't can his decisions can be perceived as recklessness? Yes, there is. When making a major decision for the organization, the leader should listen to the counsel of his fears. However, he must not make the decision solely on the counsel of his fears. He must gather all the information and facts he will need. Once he makes the decision to go forward, he must dismiss all of his fears and proceed full speed ahead. In other words, a leader doesn't let fear direct his decisions, but instead he directs the fear. This is essential to conquering fear.

Fear is a natural challenge for leaders. Most leaders struggle with fear at one time or another. Fear is one of the more difficult enemies that a leader faces. It prevents him from moving forward, making necessary changes, taking advantage of opportunities, and being a clear-thinking leader when making decisions. What are some of the things that leaders fear?

- **Failure**. No leader wants to fail, nor do they start out to fail. However, the fear of failure for a leader is very real. The fear of failure won't stop a leader from dreaming but it will stop him from pursuing the dream. The fear of failure always has a leader ask the question, "What if it doesn't work?"

- **Risk**. Many leaders want the rewards but they don't want the risk. The only problem is that risk and reward are joined at the hip. Some leaders fear the risk of taking a chance. This fear keeps leaders from making things happen. They just sit still and hope something happens.

- **Rejection**. Most leaders want to be loved and accepted by those they lead. The fear of rejection will cause a leader to go overboard in seeking to get along with everyone and not rub anyone the wrong way. When this fear is present, the leader cannot lead effectively because he will be hesitant to discipline, make corrections, confront, or hold people accountable when necessary.

Brian Tracy gives some insight on the issue of conquering fear when he says, "You must do the thing that you fear until the fear of that thing becomes no more." There are action steps that a leader can take to overcome his fears. I have listed five:

- **Confront your fears**. This is where you call your fears out to the fight. You face them like David faced Goliath. This step is where victory is won or lost. When you confront your fears, you find out that most of the threats coming from your fears were bogus.
- **Mute the voice of fear**. This is where you make fear take a back seat and you ignore every thought and voice that is not aligned with your vision. Fear is still talking, you are just not listening. You refuse to hear what fear is saying.
- **Change your belief system**. Your belief system is the driving force behind your fears. Get a checkup from the neck up. This is where you start thinking differently and therefore you start acting differently. You change from functioning in fear to functioning in faith.
- **Declare that you are going to conquer the fear**. There is tremendous power in the spoken word. What we do and what we become are many times connected to what we say. You have to speak bolder and louder than your fears.
- **Begin to do the thing you fear until the fear disappears**. Action dispels fear. The more action you apply, the more the fear dissipates. When you sit still, you allow fear the time to paralyze your abilities and efforts.

In the midst of the Great Depression, President Franklin D. Roosevelt said, "We have nothing to fear but fear itself." He was essentially saying if we can't shake our pessimistic economic outlook, it will be tough to turn things around. President Roosevelt gives a powerful lesson to leaders. Unless you realize that the only thing you have to fear is fear itself, you won't take the bold steps necessary to lead the organization into greatness.

13

Goals

"Know your goal, make a plan and pull the trigger."

—Phil C. McGraw

"Obstacles are those frightful things you see when you take your eyes off your goals."

—Sydney Smith

"The tragedy of life doesn't lie in not reaching your goal. The tragedy lies in having no goals to reach."

—Benjamin Mayes

"Shoot for the moon, even if you miss, you'll land amongst the stars."

—Les Brown

Goals are objectives to desired outcomes. They are the purpose to which an endeavor is directed. A leader must not only have goals for his life, but also for the organization or group that he is leading. The goals must center on the objectives of the organization or group. The process of setting goals allows a leader to choose where he wants to go in life. Once the leader knows what he wants to achieve, he then knows where to concentrate his efforts. Having goals allows him to spot potential distractions that would lure him off course.

Why should a leader set goals? There are several reasons for this. Goals give the leader a target in which to aim. Not setting goals is like throwing darts into thin air with no board. Goals help a leader to establish priorities and also provide motivation.

A leader's time and effort must be channeled in the right direction. In other words, he must major on the majors and minor on the minors. Goals allow the leader to do this. A key component to achieving goals is focus. Focus allows you to direct disciplined action towards your goals. Focus keeps you doing two things. First, it keeps you from veering to the left or right. By this, I mean it keeps you from getting sidetracked. Many leaders have come short of achieving their goals because they allowed things to divert their focus. Secondly, it keeps them from looking back. You can never go forward if you are looking behind you. Looking back can be a fatal mistake that leaders must avoid. As the old saying goes, "Never look back unless you are planning to go that way."

A leader must not allow obstacles to impede his progress. He must be filled with determination and tenacity to reach his goals. He must also have a plan of action to reach those goals. You must plan your work and work your plan. Having no plan is a plan to fail. In order to accomplish your goals, you must proceed with purposeful action. Success in reaching your goals is not a spectator sport; it requires your full participation. A useful way of making goals more powerful is to use the SMART mnemonic. While there are plenty of variants, SMART usually stands for:

> **S** = **Specific**. Clearly define what we are going to do.
> **M** = **Measurable**. If you can't measure it, you can't manage it.
> **A** = **Attainable**. It stretches you, but you can do it.
> **R** = **Realistic**. Not easy, but doable.
> **T** = **Timely**. Clear timeframe to work towards.[8]

The concept of SMART goals is very important to a leader accomplishing his goals. Goal setting is a powerful way to motivate a leader. Goal setting is absolutely necessary for a leader's success. In setting goals, a leader must challenge himself and commit wholeheartedly to achieving them. Effective goal setting involves creating a written strategy as to how goals will be reached. The leader establishes checkpoints along the way to chart progress both short-term and long-term. The best way to achieve this is through SMART goals.

The goals that the leader sets for the organization become much easier to attain if the leader gets the followers to buy into the goals. John Maxwell calls this the law of the buy in. The leader can assist himself with the buy in by the following steps as he sets the goals:

- **Write down the goals**. This creates a roadmap to the organization's success. It keeps the goals in front of the people for constant review. This is one of the most important steps in the goal setting process.

- **Establish an action plan.** This is the strategy to accomplish the goals. The action plan gives specific responsibilities to the team members and assists in establishing systems of accountability.
- **Set priorities.** This places the goals in the order of importance. Attention can be directed towards the most important goals. Use the number system on the goals. Give them numbers from 1 to 10 with 10 being the highest priority.
- **Reward achievements.** As goals are reached, there should be rewards for those achievements. People work harder and work together better when they realize that there will be rewards as goals are reached.

Accountability is a key ally to a leader as he pursues goals. Leaders should find someone or several persons to hold them accountable relative to the goals they have set. This should be done in conjunction with creating a system where the leader holds himself accountable. All goals begin with a dream but are maintained with desire. The dream is translated into clear definable details which coincide with the leader's goals. The details of the goals are so clear you can feel and sense them. You know what it is going to feel like when you achieve them. Desire is the fuel that keeps the leader moving toward his goals in the face of opposition and resistance.

The journey to reaching goals will have its setbacks, frustrations, and disappointments. However, the leader must find the resolve to enjoy the trip. The thing that makes the destination more rewarding is the journey to getting there. So on your way to your goals, smile, laugh, and most of all have fun.

14

Greatness

"None, but people of strong passion are capable of rising to greatness."
—Comte de Mirabeau

"Great and good are seldom the same man."
—Winston Churchill

"Great people are meteors designed to burn so that the earth may be lighted."
—Napoleon Bonaparte.

"No man is truly great who is great only in his lifetime. The test of greatness is the page of history."
—William Hazlitt

Greatness can be defined in different ways. In this case, it can be defined as a goal one strives to achieve. In golf, Tiger Woods has set his goal to surpass Jack Nicklaus' record of eighteen (18) major titles. For Tiger Woods, nineteen (19) major titles would be greatness. It can also be defined as an epic event accomplished by an individual or a team. When Martin Luther King, Jr., led the march on Washington and delivered the famous *"I Have a Dream"* speech, he was thrust into greatness. Muhammad Ali's upset victory over Sonny Liston, in their 1964 heavyweight title fight, thrust Ali into greatness. Greatness can also be defined by an invention or discovery that brings change and breakthrough to society. Microsoft founders Bill Gates' and Paul Allen's introduction of Windows changed computer technology and thrust them into greatness. The emergence of Apple's iPod (which changed how we listen to music), iPhone (which revolutionized the cell phone), and the iPad (which introduced tablet technology to the world), thrust Steve Jobs into greatness.

Leaders achieve greatness in a couple of ways. Some achieve greatness by the works and deeds they accomplish, while others are thrust into greatness by a cause that they undertake. Leaders should not be afraid to seek to attain greatness or seek to become great leaders. The only way a leader can be the very best that he can possibly become is to reach for the highest star. In leadership, that star is greatness. To seek to be a great leader is not arrogant or prideful. It represents confidence and determination. However, no leader anoints himself with greatness. Greatness is something that others bestow upon him. Greatness does not stand alone; it is interwoven and held up by five components:

- **Strong Motivation**. This gets you going. Great leaders are self-motivated. They don't need to be pumped up and jump started. They have an inner drive that keeps them motivated. With great leaders, the issue is never getting them motivated but rather slowing them down.
- **Undying Passion**. This keeps you going. Great leaders are fueled by their passion. It is their energy. It is also contagious. Their passion burns twenty-four hours a day. You can see it all over them and in everything they do.
- **Focused Ambition**. This keeps you on course. Great leaders have mastered the art of staying focused. They don't allow themselves to get distracted by having their hands in too many things. They keep the main thing the main thing.
- **Inspiring Vision**. This keeps the goal in front of you. Great leaders have a clear picture of where they are going. Their vision consumes their entire being. Every decision they make is made with their vision in mind.
- **Tenacious Perseverance**. This keeps you from giving up. Great leaders have a never-quit attitude. Quitting is against their very nature. They find strength where others give up. They always feel that victory is just over the horizon.

Greatness does not come without hard work, commitment, and discipline. Tiger Woods is a textbook example of this. His father introduced him to golf at the extremely early age of 18 months, and encouraged him to practice intensely. Tiger Woods had racked up at least 15 years of practice by the time he became the youngest-ever winner of the U.S. Amateur Championship, at age 18. He has never stopped trying to improve, devoting many hours a day to conditioning and practice, even remaking his swing twice because that's what it took to get even better.

Olympic athletes train and prepare themselves all of their lives to get to the elite status of being a gold medal winner. Leaders are always in training for their moment. Unlike an Olympic athlete who knows exactly the game, event, or moment in which he will compete, the leader does not know when his moment will come. This is why he must take his training seriously and maintain a state of readiness at all times. That way, when his moment comes, he will be ready. There is an old saying, "Unless a man has trained himself for his chance, the chance will only make him look ridiculous" (William Matthews).

Greatness should be the goal of every leader. In order to reach greatness, it means the leader has broken the gravitational pull of average and is leading at the highest level. It means you are something that others look at and admire. A perfect example of building greatness is Coach Nick Saban, the head football coach at the University of Alabama. In the years prior to Coach Saban's arrival, Alabama's once proud program was mired in a condition of mediocrity. Coach Saban came in and made returning the Crimson Tide to greatness his goal. As of this writing, in seven short years, Coach Saban has Alabama on top of the college football world. It's Alabama and everybody else. He won three BCS National Championships in a four year span. He has built a dynasty at University of Alabama that shows no signs of slowing down. Coaches across America are copying Coach Saban's system to build their programs. This only happened because greatness was the goal and Coach Saban would accept nothing less. His players have bought into his philosophy and the rest is history.

Challenges produce opportunities for greatness. Great leaders are always looking for the next challenge to thrust them to the next level of greatness. When times are stable and secure, no one is ever severely tested. But it is in adverse and challenging times that great leaders emerge. The pattern that you will notice among exemplary leaders is that they served during times of turbulence, conflict, innovation, and change. They are always associated with a challenge. When we look at the extraordinary challenges that society faces today, we can only conclude that the potential for greatness is monumental.

15

Habits

"Motivation is what gets you started. Habit is what keeps you going."

—Jim Ryun

"First we make our habits, then our habits make us."

—Charles C. Noble

"Everything you are used to, once done long enough, starts to seem natural, even though it might not be"

—Julien Smith

"Habit is either the best of servants or the worst of masters."

—Nathaniel Emmons

A habit is a pattern of behavior acquired through frequent repetition. It is routine and oftentimes an established custom or behavior that one does without thinking. It is so regularly followed that it becomes almost involuntary. All great leaders, if they are honest, will tell you they have both good and bad habits. However, their good habits far outweigh their bad habits. They do not allow bad habits to dominate their lives. Instead, their lives are models of routine, established behaviors that amount to good habits. This is what causes us to emulate and follow them.

It is imperative that a leader develop good habits. As a matter of fact, you can observe the habits of a leader and from those habits accurately predict his level of success. What are good habits? Good habits are habits that produce positive action and positive benefits. A leader must have the fortitude to break the bad habits in his life that are obstacles to his success and effectiveness as a leader. Many leaders with enormous potential have sabotaged their own success with bad habits that they would not or could not conquer. The leadership graveyard is filled with gifted and talented leaders whose enormous potential was short-circuited by an enemy known as "bad habits."

Successful leaders become successful because they develop good habits. In the book, *Seven Habits of Highly Effective People,* Steven Covey identifies the habits of successful and effective people. In taking a page from Covey, I have observed the habits of successful leaders that I have had the privilege to know on a personal level and have come up with Wilder's "Seven Habits of Successful Leaders."

- **Positive Attitude**. This is a habit that a leader can't afford to leave home without. Successful leaders make it a habit to always be positive even in the face of negative circumstances. This habit makes or breaks a leader.

- **Life Long Learners**. This is a habit that keeps successful leaders growing. They are always trying to get better and seeking ways to improve. They read continually, because successful leaders are readers. All great leaders understand that they must read to grow and keep the edge.

- **Remove Limitations**. This is a habit that allows leaders to do what many thought could not be done. Successful leaders refuse to accept limitations. They laugh when they are told what they cannot do. They are fearless in their pursuit of reaching whatever they aim for.

- **Accept Responsibility**. This habit shows the maturity of a leader. Successful leaders don't have a victim complex. They understand that being the leader means ultimately being responsible for the successes and failures of the organization. They don't pass the buck.

- **Build Great Teams**. This habit allows leaders to surround themselves with great people. They recruit the best and brightest talent to be a part of their team. They build a strong inner circle of people who are strong where they are weak. Leaders who develop this habit are not insecure.

- **Ignore Critics**. This habit shows the focus of a leader. Successful leaders don't spend time dialoging with their critics or allowing them to set their agenda. They use their critics as fuel for their fire. They understand that having critics is a part of the success journey.

- **Reward Achievement**. This habit allows leaders to honor those who serve under their leadership. This makes people love them and desire to serve them.

Successful leaders always see that there is a reward system for the achievers in the organization. If you want people to give you their best, reward them for their achievements.

My observations have shown me that leaders who develop these habits are successful. The development of these habits can bring success to any leader who commits to practice them in his life. In reading a book titled, *Thinking For A Change* by John Maxwell, I came across the following statement that had a profound impact on me. It said:

> "I am your constant companion. I am your greatest helper or your heaviest burden. I will push you onward or drag you down to failure. I am completely at your command. Half the things you do, you might just as well turn over to me and I will be able to do them quickly and correctly. I am easily managed; you must merely be firm with me. Show me exactly how you want something done and after a few lessons, I will do it automatically.

> I am the servant of all great men; and, alas, of all failures as well. Those who are great, I have made great. Those who are failures, I have made failures. I am not a machine, though I work with all the precision of a machine plus the intelligence of a man. You may run me for profit or run me for ruin, it makes no difference to me. Take me, train me, be firm with me and I will put the world at your feet. Be easy with me, and I will destroy you. Who am I? I am habit!"[9]

16

Influence

"The measure of a man is what he does with his power."

—Pittacus

"The key to successful leadership today is influence, not authority."

—Kenneth Blanchard

"The greatest ability in business is to get along with others and to influence their actions."

—John Hancock

"A leader is one who influences a specific group of people to move in a God-given direction."

—J. Robert Clinton

Influence is a term that refers to the ability to indirectly control or affect the actions of other people or things. Influence means that someone is following you and being impacted by you. If no one is following you, you are not leading. The ancient Chinese proverb says, "He who thinks he leads and has no one following him is only taking a walk."

Influence is a powerful tool in the hands of a leader. A leader is given tremendous influence over organizations and the lives of people. This is a sacred trust. A leader must never allow his influence to become control. When this happens, there is a total breakdown of the integrity of the relationship between the leader and the followers. The most important quality a person of influence has is integrity with people. A leader is on different levels of influence with those he leads, therefore, he must be aware of his level of influence with people.

Mastering the art of influence is the key to success in leadership. For example, he may be on level five influence with one person and level two influence with another. The manner in which he communicates, what he demands, and how he relates to individuals is determined by the level of influence he has. A critical mistake leaders make is when they attempt to push a level two person like a level five, sometimes the damage done is irreparable. To be an effective leader, it is necessary to influence others to support and implement decisions that the leader deems necessary for the success of the group or organization.

Without influence, leadership does not occur. If force has to be used to get people to go along with you, it is not leadership, it is authoritarianism. Leadership is not force or coercion. As John Maxwell says, "Leadership is influence." The effective leaders are experts at influencing the followers to the desired outcome. Leaders can't change people, but they can influence them. Let's look at a leader's acronym for influence:

I. A leader is an **initiator** who makes things happen. Things are always moving around them.

N. A leader **never** stops growing. Leaders are lifelong learners.

F. A leader is **flexible** and open to change. Leaders are change agents.

L. A leader **leads** by example in all things. First and foremost, leaders lead.

U. A leader **understands** that the right people are his greatest asset. Leaders are not lone rangers.

E. A leader **equips** his followers to **excel**. Leaders help followers succeed.

N. A leader embraces **new** ideas and methods for improvement. Leaders are innovators.

C. A leader is a **coach** who always has a game plan. Leaders are strategic thinkers.

E. A leader is driven by his quest for **excellence**. Leaders see average as the enemy.

There is no real leadership without influence. If a leader is leading and he has no influence, then the people are following him because they have to. When a leader has influence, people follow because they want to. The major difference between the two is production. When people follow because they have to, the leader will never get their best, they will not go beyond their job description. You can pull rank and coerce obedience with authority, but you will lose influence.

However, when people follow because they are influenced, not only will the leader get their best, he will get their heart. When this happens, the leader has gained power and trust with the followers. Great influencers have great interaction with the followers because they understand you cannot effectively influence in isolation. Influence requires and demands interaction. You cannot have impact unless you have contact.

We have stated that leadership is influence. That raises the question, "Does all influence count as leadership?" Not necessarily, it depends on how the influence is used. For example, a criminal might influence someone through bribery as a means of achieving an objective. A swift talking salesman can influence someone to buy something they may not have intended to buy. However, neither of these is leadership. Influence becomes leadership when purpose is the fuel that's driving it. In the two examples given, purpose is not involved, they are totally self-serving. In true leadership, however, influence is used to direct the group or followers toward the purpose and goals of the organization. Influence should always be used to build towards something that is larger than the leader and serves a greater purpose.

17

Integrity

"Have the courage to say no. Have the courage to face the truth. Do the right thing because it is right. These are the magic keys to living your life with integrity."
—W. Clement Stone

"The supreme quality for a leader is unquestionably integrity."
—Dwight D. Eisenhower

"If you have integrity, nothing else matters. If you don't have integrity, nothing else matters."
—Alan Simpson

"Integrity is not a 90 percent thing, not a 95 percent thing; either you have it or you don't."
—Peter Scotese

Integrity is the quality or condition of being whole, complete, unbroken, and undivided. It means that you are true to yourself and to your values. Integrity is what you do when no one is watching, that there is no gap between what you say and what you do. In leadership, there is no greater a characteristic than integrity. It is the keystone of leadership. To a leader, integrity is about doing what is right rather than what is convenient. It is knowing the difference between right and wrong and what is ethical and unethical...and then doing what is right and ethical.

There are many ways to define integrity. I like Waldo Waldman's definition of integrity in his article, *The Price of Integrity – The most important building block of a successful business and life.* He says integrity means:

- Honoring your commitments.
- Being a man or woman of your word.
- Doing the right thing (even when no-one is watching).
- Admitting when you mess up (and accepting the consequences).
- Never sacrificing your relationships or honor for money.[10]

How does a leader develop integrity as part of his character? Where does integrity come from? Leaders are not naturally born with integrity, but rather it is learned and developed throughout one's life. Leaders will constantly be faced with decisions and circumstances where their integrity will be tested. General Ronald R. Fogleman wrote in his article, *The Leadership-Integrity Link*, "I believe you build a lifestyle of integrity one step at a time. Individual acts of integrity lead to a habit of integrity, and individual habits add up to a way of life. Simplistic? Perhaps so, but I've never found a more effective way of developing personal integrity than by applying it to everything you do, every day of your life—no matter how small or seemingly inconsequential the matter at hand. Since organizations tend to take on the personality of their leadership, building integrity must start at the top. Dishonest acts are like cancers that eat at the moral fiber of organizations, especially if the acts are explicitly or implicitly condoned by leaders."[11] Leaders must act with integrity at all times. There cannot be lapses of judgment or compromises of values which will begin to erode one's integrity. The entire organization from the top to the bottom suffers when there is a lack of integrity in the leader. Can a leader regain his integrity if he stumbles and loses it? Yes, in time he can gain back his integrity; however, he may not gain back all the trust he lost in the process. Integrity alone will not make a person a leader; however, without it, the leader will absolutely not be a good leader. Integrity is the foundation of leadership. It is what leaders stand upon; it is how they are maintained. When a leader lacks this foundation, at some point his leadership crashes before him. We have seen this happen in the field of politics, business, sports, education, and unfortunately, religion in recent years.

One of the more tragic examples of a leader losing his integrity is John Edwards, the former U.S. senator from North Carolina. Senator Edwards was a very talented and gifted politician who rose up swiftly through the ranks of the Democratic Party. In 2003, he mounted his first campaign for the presidency. A strong showing in the primaries earned him a spot as John Kerry's running mate in 2004. Although Kerry lost the presidential election to President George W. Bush, Edwards became a front runner for the Democratic Party nomination for president in 2008.

However, Edwards' presidential aspirations came crumbling down in early 2008 when it was revealed that he had fathered a child in an extramarital affair while his wife, Elizabeth, battled incurable cancer. He was also accused of scheming to use wealthy donors' money to help him cover up his affair and hide his mistress from the public. After a federal investigation into his campaign finances, Edwards was indicted by a federal grand jury in North Carolina on six criminal charges of violating federal campaign-finance law.

Although Edwards was acquitted on one charge and a mistrial declared on the five other charges, his fall from grace was complete. He went off the national scene into oblivion to be remembered no more as a meaningful politician. A once promising politician's political career was derailed because of a lack of integrity. His is a classic example of a person's talents and gifts taking them to a place that their character could not keep them.

Integrity is not something that comes automatically to a leader. Actions that demonstrate the possession of integrity are intentional. Integrity consists of several components:

- **Honesty**. This means that there are no contradictions or discrepancies in your thoughts, words, or actions. A leader with integrity is truthful and does not engage in deceitfulness.
- **Responsibility**. This means accepting that you and you alone are responsible for your life. This comes with the realization that you are what you are and where you are because of your own conduct and behavior.
- **Accountability**. This means the readiness or preparedness to give an explanation or justification to superiors and significant others for your actions. Leaders who want to do the right thing welcome accountability. Only dishonest leaders detest accountability.

- **Principle**. This means to have a standard of good behavior, moral standards, and ethical behavior that guides your conduct and practice. A leader should be a person of principle.
- **Values.** These are the concepts that govern our behavior. They represent our highest priorities and deeply held driving forces. The core values of a leader define who and what the leader is.

Integrity demonstrated by a leader causes people to trust the leader and believe in his leadership. There is one very important fact about integrity, and that is it cannot be taken from you. You have to give it up. It is an issue of the choice or choices you make. You might be influenced, manipulated, or coerced, but ultimately you must make the choice to do something unethical or immoral that bring about the loss of your integrity. If faced with the decision, it is better to lose friends and associates than to lose your integrity. The justification for this is they are much easier to replace than your integrity.

18

Judgment

"Courage is not the absence of fear, but rather the judgment that something else is more important than fear."

—Ambrose Redmoon

"Good judgment comes from experience. Experience comes from bad judgment."

—Rita Mae Brown

"Judge a tree from its fruit, not from its leaves"

—Euripides

"Failure is simply a few errors in judgment, repeated every day."

—Jim Rohn

Judgment is the capacity to form an opinion by distinguishing, evaluating, and assessing situations or circumstances and drawing sound conclusions. One of the most important roles that a leader has is making good judgments. His decisions must be wise and well informed. This produces positive results for the organization. Nothing is more central to his function as leader than good judgment. When the leader consistently shows good judgment, the organization prospers and all other issues seem minute. When the leader has a track record of poor judgment, the organization suffers and all other issues are magnified.

No leader can make the right judgment calls one hundred percent of the time. However, the highly successful leaders make the right judgments a high percentage of the time, especially when it counts the most. A leader's judgment is important because the success or failure of the organization is dependent upon it. On a personal level, each individual leader's quality of life and accomplishments in life will depend upon his judgment.

Research seems to suggest that a leader's judgment is most important in two areas—people and strategy. With respect to people, he must get the right people on his team to help him and the organization succeed. Choosing people is always a judgment call. It is sometimes risky, but absolutely necessary. In his book, *Good to Great*, Jim Collins alludes to the idea that the great leaders get the people correct first. The executives who ignited the transformations from good to great did not first figure out where to drive the bus and then get people to take it there. No, they first got the right people on the bus (and the wrong people off the bus) and then figured out where to drive it. They in essence said, "Look, I don't really know where we should take this bus. But I know this much: If we get the right people on the bus, the right people in the right seats, and the wrong people off the bus, then we'll figure out how to take it someplace great."[12]

The issue of strategy involves how to accomplish the organization's objectives and vision. Leaders have led businesses into wrong strategies that cost them their market share and their place in the business world. Some companies never recover from bad strategy. On the flipside, there have been leaders whose judgment chose a strategy that some questioned as sound strategy, but in the end, it was highly successful and propelled the company to greatness. If you were to study great leaders in comparison to leaders who failed, you will find one major difference; the great leaders consistently made good judgment calls; the failed leaders had a track record of poor judgment calls.

Great leaders make great judgment calls because they have good intuition. They have developed it to the point that they trust it fully. It is like a sixth sense to them. Excellent decisions don't just happen by accident. There are factors involved in making good decisions. When a leader is faced with making a judgment call, there are several things he must consider:

- **What the facts at hand are telling him**. He must carefully and correctly analyze the facts. There are leaders who ignore the facts hoping that they will just go away. This is poor judgment. A leader must acknowledge the facts no matter how brutal they are.
- **What his intuition is telling him.** Intuition is the ability to acquire knowledge without inference or the use of reason. Sometimes his intuition will tell him to do the opposite of what the facts tell him to do. Good leaders learn to trust their intuition.

- **Have all options been weighed**. No stone must be left unturned; every possible option must be considered. Without all the options before him, the leader's ability to make a sound judgment call could be compromised. He needs a clear picture of all that is before him.
- **What the ramifications of his call will be**. He must come to terms with the impact his call will have on the organization and the lives of other people. This is the real burden of leadership.

It is not easy making decisions, especially judgment calls, however, they must be made and it is the leader's job to make them. The higher the leader is in the organization, the greater impact the judgment call will have on the organization and the lives of the people involved. That is why we have leaders. In their book, *Judgment: How Winning Leaders Make Great Calls*, Tichy and Bennis state it plainly, "What can be said for sure is that judgment is the core, the nucleus of leadership. And that in decision making, the only thing that counts is winning or losing. The results matter—nothing else."[13]

19

Knowledge

"Anyone who stops learning is old, whether at twenty or eighty. Anyone who keeps learning stays young."

—Henry Ford

"Knowledge has to be improved, challenged, and increased constantly, or it vanishes."

—Peter F. Drucker

"Live as if you were to die tomorrow. Learn as if you were to live forever."

—Mahatma Gandhi

"Be curious always, for knowledge will not acquire you; you must acquire it."

—Sudie Back

The Oxford English Dictionary defines knowledge as the expertise and skills acquired by a person through experience or education. It is also defined as the theoretical or practical understanding of a subject. A leader is one who knows. He should have acquired knowledge either through experience, education or both. He is the leader because he knows more than those following him. They depend upon his knowledge for their success and the organization's success. When the organization faces a crisis, the leader is expected to possess the knowledge to lead them out of it. In short, a leader has to know.

He should have abundant knowledge about the industry in which he operates. Followers expect the leader to know and have an answer for every problem. It never enters their mind that he may not know something or not have an answer. I remember as my children were growing up, we would turn the television on to look at a movie. We would sit down together at the same time and turn on the movie. Many times, though, when we actually began to watch it, the movie would already be in the middle. My children would ask me what happened up to that point. It never occurred to them that I sat down with them and started watching the movie the same time they did, yet, because I was Daddy, the leader in their eyes, they expected me to know what was happening in the movie.

It is the same way in every branch of leadership, whether business, government, religious, educational, etc.; the leader is expected to know and have an answer. There are times when the leader has to utter those three words that no follower wants to hear, "I don't know." Not knowing something isn't a problem. The problem occurs when the leader remains in a state of not knowing. Every leader should have people in his circle of relationships that can provide the answers he needs. Knowledge is an essential part of a leader's ability to lead, innovate, and to be successful in the organization he is leading. There are several things that a leader should know:

- **A leader should know his field** *(Business)*. Whatever the field, a leader must be an expert in it. He should know the trends and changes taking place in his field. His knowledge of the field is one of the things that qualifies him to be the leader. A leader's knowledge of his field is invaluable to his organization or company. A leader cannot take a shortcut here. In this area, he must always stay at the top of his game. He should always be in a mode of continuing education in his field of expertise.

- **A leader should know his followers** *(People)*. People are the greatest asset a leader has; therefore, it behooves him to have a keen knowledge of the people he is leading. He must know their strengths and weaknesses, what they are capable of doing and what they are not capable of doing. He must know how to motivate them in order to get the best out of them. He has to communicate his genuine care and concern for them. It has been said that people don't care how much you know until they know how much you care.

- **A leader must know how to lead in times of crises** *(Critical Moments)*. Every organization will go through times of crisis. Leadership is critical during these times. There are four basic elements to leading in a time of crisis. These include (1) being visible and available, (2) communicating supportively, carefully and regularly, (3) controlling one's behavior and reactions, and (4) giving the situation perspective to create alignment.[14] In times of crisis, the leader has to be a source of strength for the organization. He cannot show signs of fear and dismay because everyone will be looking to him for stability. These times are his greatest leadership moments.

- **A leader must know how to manage failure (Disappointment).** No company has ever batted a thousand in all of its strategic implementation. Some failed miserably. The leader must know how to manage the failure when the strategy has not worked, momentum is slowed, and morale is low. The leader must help the followers to see that failure provides a great learning opportunity, and that it is only through seeming failure that most of life's greatest successes are achieved. He must know how to lead them from defeat to victory.

As it regards a leader's knowledge, Clarence B. Randall put it best when he said, "The leader must know, must know that he knows, and must be able to make it abundantly clear to those about him that he knows." People expect the leader to know and as the leader you can't let them down. Randall's point is made clear in the movie U-571. Thrust into the position as leader when the captain is killed in battle, the newly appointed captain (played by Matthew McConaughey) of a navy submarine that is under heavy torpedo fire is asked by members of his crew what they were going to do. He replied, "You think I have all the answers, I don't know."

His second in command, (played by Harvey Keitel) is an older naval officer who has been around a while, when alone with the captain requested permission to speak freely. The captain granted his request and he said, "This is the navy, where a commanding officer is a mighty and terrible thing, a man to be feared and respected. All knowing, all powerful. Don't you dare say what you said to the boys back there again; 'I don't know.' Those three words will kill a crew, dead as the depth charge. You're the skipper now, and the skipper always knows what to do, whether he does or not."

20

Leadership

"A leader is a dealer in hope."
—Napoleon Bonaparte

"A leader is one who knows the way, goes the way, and shows the way."
—John Maxwell

"The secret of a leader lies in the tests he has faced over the whole course of his life and the habit of action he develops in meeting those tests."
—Gail Sheehy

"A leader takes people where they want to go. A great leader takes people where they don't necessarily want to go, but ought to be."
—Rosalynn Carter

The primary function of a leader is to provide leadership. In his role as leader, he must delegate many things, but the one thing he cannot delegate is the providing of leadership within the organization. He is the leader and must lead in every sense of the word. He is the one who must make the team go. In football, the quarterback is the team leader. He is the one who makes plays and makes the team go. He doesn't become a leader when the coach makes him the quarterback; he becomes the quarterback because he is already a leader. The same is true in organizational institutions. The leader does not become the leader when he is given a position of leadership; he is given the position of leadership because he is already a leader. If he cannot make the calls a leader should make, he will not be the leader very long. If he cannot lead the team, his value to the team diminishes because every successful team must have a leader.

What leadership skills must the leader demonstrate? There are many skills required of leaders and all of them are necessary and valuable. However, I will emphasize three: vision, delegation and motivation.

1. **Vision**. A leader must have peripheral vision. A leader must be one who sees it all. He must keep his eyesight sharp and polished. A leader does not have the luxury of times and seasons of temporary blindness. If this happens, the entire organization suffers. There is nothing worse than a blind leader. Leaders who cannot see are leading their organization on a Titanic course. There are three kinds of sight that a leader must have:

   • **Hindsight**. A leader must have the correct perception of things or events after they have happened in order to learn and grow from them.

- **Insight**. A leader must be able to see into a situation and apprehend the inner nature of that situation in order to properly respond to it.
- **Foresight**. A leader must possess the ability to look forward and see ahead. This allows him to foresee potential problems, as well as see and seize opportunities.

2. **Delegation**. Leaders must learn how to get things done through people. There are two main reasons for delegation. First, the ability to delegate frees the leader from the tasks that consume energy and skills that could be better utilized in more essential matters. Delegation is only effective when the leader delegates properly. This involves choosing a person who has the skills to carry out the task given to him. Therefore, the leader must choose carefully and skillfully those to whom he delegates assignments. Second, delegation helps to develop the team members. It shows that the leader places confidence in their ability to complete the task. It allows them to grow and develop their skills. Delegation will ultimately give the team members a broader set of skills than they had before.

3. **Motivation**. The ability to motivate is one of the most valuable qualities a leader should possess. If the followers are not motivated by the leader, success is virtually impossible. One of the greatest assets any organization can have is motivated people. Leaders are responsible for creating an environment that motivates the team members to accomplish the goals of the organization. One of the more difficult challenges to a leader is to learn how to effectively motivate those who support him. One of the reasons it is so difficult

is because motivation can be extremely personal. What motivates one person may not motivate the next person. Good leaders understand the different dynamics needed to motivate different people. To keep the team motivated, the leader must constantly remind them of the organization's vision, hold them accountable to the established goals, mentor and coach them on improving their skills, and give them the support in their work that they will need to succeed.

These are just three of the skills that leadership requires. Remember, first and foremost, the leader must lead. That is the reason he is hired or appointed. He is not the manager; he is the leader. The difference between leaders and managers is that managers are responsible for maintaining the status quo. It's their job to keep the wheels turning, whereas, leaders are responsible for vision and strategy. They decide which wheels to turn. Managers are like thermometers; they tell the temperature. Leaders are like thermostats; they set the temperature. Managers manage things, while leaders lead people. No one has ever been called a world manager, but there are some called world leaders.

Leadership in action is a beautiful art. If there were no classes on leadership or no books on leadership to be read, one could learn leadership just by watching great leaders in action as they practice their art. You would learn principles that would be invaluable to you because great leaders practice and live by principles. Here are a few principles that great leaders live by:

- **Take responsibility for his and the team's actions**. Great leaders do not shift responsibility to others. They stand and face the music. Sometimes, leaders have to take responsibility for the actions of their subordinates.

Is this fair? In leadership, you accept the fact that it comes with the territory. The buck stops with the leader. Nothing kills morale within the team more than the leader blaming the team for failure to reach a goal or shortcomings in production.

- **Keep growing as a leader.** Successful leaders maintain a learning posture throughout their lives. They are lifelong learners. To them, leadership is not an event but rather a journey. A journey that has no end. They never come to a place in leadership where they feel that they have arrived. Their mindset is such that no matter how great they become as a leader, there is still room to grow. The secret to their success is that they never stop growing.

- **Lead by example.** Leadership is about being out in the front and modeling the behavior and standard that is expected of the followers. Modeling refers to a representation made to be copied, or more generally to any person or thing to be followed or imitated because of excellence. In leadership, more is caught than taught. The followers will catch more from the example you set for them than what you teach in a classroom. With them, it is not the old saying, "Don't do as I do, but do as I say." With them it is, "Do what you see me do."

- **Make good decisions.** As noted in an earlier chapter, leadership involves making decisions. Some of the decisions are challenging and critical. This is the one area that can make or break one's leadership tenure. There have been leaders who have been removed from their position as leader because of bad or poor decisions. Great leaders are decisive. They are not muddled and indeterminate. The leader must learn to balance emotion with reason when making decisions. Making decisions is not easy but is an absolutely essential part of leadership.

- **Develop the team**. Helping others to grow and improve their skills is a role in leadership that every leader must embrace. The development process involves identifying and preparing the next generation of leaders. Great leaders and successful companies intentionally identify and develop leaders for the future. As the leader develops the team, productivity goes up, goals are met, strategy is executed, morale is high, the team performs at a higher level, and the leader is rewarded for his achievements with the team. In sports, there is a saying that the coach coached the players up, meaning that he made them greater in the end. A leader must lead the followers up. The leader must make them better leaders in the end than when they came to him.

As the leader, you must lead with passion and energy. People will feed off the passion and the energy that the leader displays. My graduate school dean at Southwestern Christian University, Dr. Garnet Pike, would remind us at the end of every class to always be on time for class because leaders lead. That phrase is the essence of leadership, "Leaders Lead."

21

Legacy

"If your actions create a legacy that inspires others to dream more, learn more, do more and become more, then, you are an excellent leader."

—Dolly Parton

"What you leave behind is not what is engraved in stone monuments, but what is woven into the lives of others."

—Pericles

"If you would not be forgotten, as soon as you are dead and rotten; either write things worthy of reading, or do things worthy of writing."

—Benjamin Franklin

"A good character is the best tombstone. Those who loved you, and were helped by you, will remember you when forget-me-nots are withered. Carve your name on hearts, and not on marble."

—Charles H. Spurgeon

A legacy is what one leaves behind. It is how one is remembered. Every leader will leave a legacy, be it good or bad. In a leader's youth, he doesn't think a lot about leaving a legacy because at that stage of his maturity, a legacy is not important to him. This is because in his youth, he feels invincible and immortal. He is thinking about conquest and conquering. However, as he ages, his legacy becomes very important to him. His perspective and his thinking changes. He realizes that he has more years behind him than before him, that time is not long on his side, and that he is in the second half of the game. His thinking begins to focus solely on his legacy, not on what he has done but rather what he will do. In other words, what really begins to matter to him is how he will finish and what he will leave behind for those who follow him.

The questions a leader begins to ask himself are, "When my work is done, what will be my contribution to the world? How will my name be remembered?" In the movie, *Troy*, Achilles (played by Brad Pitt) is preparing to fight a huge Thessalonian warrior when a young boy who admires him says to Achilles, "He is the biggest man I have ever seen. I would never fight him." Achilles answers him by saying, "That is why no one will remember your name." What Achilles was saying to the young boy is that you will leave no legacy. When we come to the end of our journey of life and begin to reminisce over it, several questions will come to our mind:

- What have I accomplished in my lifetime? Did I reach my potential?
- What impact did I have on those I led? Did I leave a mark on their hearts?
- Who will take my place? Did I properly train and prepare them?

- Can the organization live, thrive, and prosper after I'm gone? Did I prepare them for a future without me?
- Is the organization in better shape upon my exit than it was upon my arrival? Did I grow it and make it strong and stable?
- How will people remember me? Will it be positive or negative?
- How will my wife and children describe my life? Will they speak of me with great pride and joy?
- How will my friends describe my life? Will they tell their grandchildren that I was a role model?
- What contributions did I make? Will my work live on after me?
- Will I be remembered and talked about twenty five years from now? Does my name live on long after I am gone?

A legacy is about greatness and immortality. If a leader is going to have a lasting legacy, he must accomplish great things such as winning a great battle (Achilles and General Patton), leading a nation in turbulent times (President Lincoln and President Roosevelt), doing great things on behalf of other people (Martin Luther King and Nelson Mandela), making a mark in the business world (Steve Jobs and Bill Gates), or performing great exploits in the field of sports (Muhammad Ali and Michael Jordan). Each of these individuals left a lasting legacy of greatness in their arena of service that assures their names will never be forgotten.

A leader's legacy will be enhanced or diminished by the way he finishes. A good finish adds to his legacy, while a bad finish takes away from his legacy. One of my graduate school professors at Southwestern Christian University, Dr. J. Robert

Clinton, did a presentation on leaders entitled, "Finishing Well." He identified several categories of finishes that leaders have. In his list, he gives Biblical characters as an example of each type of finish. I have also added a U.S. President to each type of finish as an example:

- **Cut off Early.** Means they were taken out of leadership (assassination, killed in battle, prophetically denounced or overthrown). Some of these were traced directly to God's doing—Biblical examples: Samson, Absalom, John the Baptist; U.S. President: John F. Kennedy.
- **Finished Poorly.** Means they were going downhill in the latter part of their leadership. This might mean in terms of their personal relationship with God or in terms of competency in their leadership role or both—Biblical examples: Gideon, Saul, Solomon; U.S. President: Richard Nixon.
- **Finished "So So".** Means they did not do what they could have done or should have done. This might mean there were some negative ramifications from their leadership which lingered on although they did good things—Biblical examples: David, Jehoshaphat, Hezekiah; U.S. President: Bill Clinton.
- **Finished Well.** Means they were walking in a high level of leadership and had realized great levels of potential. In the end, they were greatly celebrated and honored—Biblical examples: Abraham, Joshua, Samuel, Daniel, Paul, Peter; U.S. President: Franklin D. Roosevelt.[15]

Leadership expert Ken Blanchard writes, "Whatever your position, if you influence the lives of those around you, you are engaged in the act of leadership. And if you are a leader in any sense, you are creating a legacy as you live your daily life. Your leadership legacy is the sum total of the difference you make in people's lives, directly and indirectly, formally and informally. Will you consciously craft your legacy or simply leave it up to chance?"[16]

Every leader will leave a legacy, and will be remembered for something or for nothing. You have the sole responsibility for your legacy. It cannot be delegated. It is yours and yours alone. Don't leave it up to chance. Leave a positive and lasting legacy. Make a mark on society and humanity that cannot be erased.

22

Mentoring

"At its core, mentoring is a relationship. However, it is not a relationship with just anyone. It is a relationship with someone who you like, enjoy, believe in, and want to see win in life."

—P. Ronald Wilder

"A good coach will make his players see what they can become rather than what they are."

—Ara Parseghian

"People seldom improve when they have no other model but themselves to copy."

—Oliver Goldsmith

"Mentoring is a brain to pick, an ear to listen, and a push in the right direction."

—John Crosby

Mentoring refers to a developmental relationship between a more experienced person, a mentor, and a less experienced partner who is referred to as a protégé—a person guided and protected by a more prominent person. The mentor in most cases is helping the protégé to do a job more effectively and/or to progress in a certain field of endeavor. Mentoring is something in which every leader can and must participate. Mentoring is one of the fundamental practices of leadership. A leader should always be mentoring and developing protégés so they can reach their highest potential. The thing that qualifies the leader to be a mentor is that he has "been there, done that." Therefore, from his experience, he is helping someone else gain the experience and knowledge to be the best they can be and to win as he has.

Mentoring is a natural part of leadership and it is all about influence. Mentoring involves the leader sharing or passing along his wisdom to someone else. It is one of the areas where a leader's true greatness can be seen because long after he has gone, his influence will still remain and live on in those he has mentored. This is how a leader begins to seal his legacy. No one has ever become a great leader without the influence of a mentor. If you do a study of the great leaders of our time, you will find that they all had someone to mentor them and prepare them for leadership.

This is true in politics, business, ministry, sports—in all areas of endeavor. The late Bill Walsh, former coach of the San Francisco 49ers, is considered to be one of the greatest coaches in NFL history. He coached the 49ers to three Super Bowl victories and he is the inventor of the "West Coast Offense." Walsh's greatness is not only seen in his coaching ability, but in all of the NFL head coaches that were produced through his mentoring. Below is a chart of the coaching lineage of Bill Walsh.

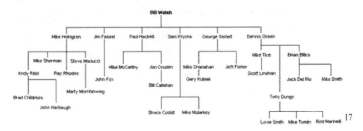

Bill Walsh is a perfect example of the power of mentoring. He retired after his third Super Bowl victory and turned the team over to one of his protégés, George Seifert, who won two more Super Bowls. Walsh has been retired from the NFL for over twenty-five years, yet his influence can still be felt in the NFL by the coaches mentored by him or those in his lineage. When a leader mentors a protégé, he is empowering the protégé to do what he does. A true mentor really wants to see his protégé surpass him. He wants his ceiling to be his protégé's floor.

Mentoring is a very unselfish act because in mentoring, the mentor is not doing it to get something back. There is no fee or expense associated with mentoring. The protégé does not promise the mentor some great financial gain for mentoring him. It is strictly a freewill act. On the other hand, there is not a more selfish act a leader can commit than to choose not to mentor those who need and seek his mentoring. In the Bible, Jesus said, *"Freely ye have received, freely give."*[18] Some helpful tips to follow when mentoring a protégé or protégés are:

- **Share your life with your protégés**. Tell them your story. Nothing is more powerful than your story. Let your life be an open book to them. Share your victories and conquests while at the same time sharing your mistakes and failures. Let them see the good, the bad, and the ugly.

- **Help your protégés to be successful.** Show them the principles and precepts that will cause them to win. Evaluate and re-evaluate the protégé to ensure that they understand the principles and precepts. Drill them until the principles become second nature. Supply them with the tools, resources, and support system to ensure their success.

- **Challenge them to get out of their comfort zones.** The greatest way to help them to grow is to stretch them beyond what is comfortable for them. A leader has to be the mother eagle. When a mother eagle is teaching her young to fly, she removes the hay and straw from the nest so that the sticks and thorns will be exposed to the young eagle and begin to stick them. The nest is no longer comfortable to them and they want to get out. Leaders must do the same to their protégés.

- **Have open, honest dialog.** Always tell them the truth, even if it hurts. Give them constructive criticism. Allow them permission to speak freely. Deal with any unresolved issues. Establish in the rules of engagement that they must always reveal their heart and true feelings. The Bible admonishes us in Ephesians 4:15 (NLT), *"Instead, we will speak the truth in love..."* You must make a commitment to deal truthfully even if the subject matter is painful.

There are numerous challenges confronting us today and in the future, but one of our greatest challenges is preparing the next generation of leaders. We have seen great movements in the past come to a screeching halt because of a failure to prepare the next generation of leaders. It has been said that everything rises and falls on leadership. If this is true, it behooves every leader to begin to identify and mentor the next generation of leaders to secure our future prosperity and advancement. Leadership development is not automatic. There must be an intentional strategy of preparing young leaders. Mentoring is that strategy.

23

Momentum

"As any athlete knows, momentum is the most unstoppable force in sports. The only way to stop it is if you get in your own way, start making stupid mistakes or stop believing in yourself."
—Rocco Mediate

"Football is a collision sport, basketball is a precision sport and volleyball is an emotional sport. You've got to get the emotion. Once you get that and the momentum behind you, there's a lot you can do."
—Mark Royer

"To create momentum in your life, never leave the scene of a decision without taking action in support of your decision no matter how insignificant the action seems..."
—William Osler

"Success requires first expending ten units of effort to produce one unit of results. Your momentum will then produce ten units of results with each unit of effort."
—Charles Givens

P. Ronald Wilder

Momentum is a physics term; it refers to the quantity of motion that an object has. In leadership, it is the forward motion that the leader has generated in the organization. Once this forward motion is moving in a positive direction, the leader will see dynamic results in his favor. Momentum is a term commonly used in sports. When a team has momentum, it means the team has things going in its favor and it will take great effort to stop it. Just as dogs are considered man's best friend, momentum is a leader's best friend. Once a leader has momentum on his side, he can seem unstoppable. It makes big problems that arise seem small and easy to conquer or overcome. When a leader doesn't have momentum on his side, it makes small problems loom large and seemingly insurmountable.

Many times, momentum is the difference between winning and losing. John Maxwell calls momentum the "great exaggerator." When you have it, people think you are better than you are. You're on a roll and everybody is amazed by your success. When you lose momentum, people think you are worse than you are. Momentum magnifies your performance and positive momentum can be a potent force to push you forward.[19]

It does not matter what type of organization you lead, one of the keys that will determine the level of your success as a leader is momentum. Momentum has also been defined as "the force of movement." It can help decide how high your organization will go and how quickly you will get there. Because momentum is such an important key to a leader's success, when he gets it, he should put forth great effort and diligence to keep it. Momentum is much easier to manage than it is to try to obtain or recapture once you have lost it. It is sometimes complex. It is here today and gone tomorrow.

There are things that a leader can do to create momentum or build on the momentum that has already been generated.

There are five life lines of momentum. If a leader builds on these, momentum will be his constant companion:

- **Clarity of Vision**. This is the womb where momentum is born because it identifies where you are going. When the vision is clear and the goals can be seen, momentum is conceived.
- **Good and Courageous Decisions**. When this happens, momentum can burst forth in an organization. Successful leaders do not sit on decisions; they make quick decisions to keep up momentum.
- **Right People**. When a leader surrounds himself with the right people, gaining momentum is very easy, almost automatic. The right people in an organization are to a leader what the sails are to a sailboat.
- **Wins Under Your Belt**. Everybody likes a winner and everybody wants to be associated with winners. Wins bring a momentum that causes the team to perform at very high levels. Celebrate every win no matter how small it is.
- **A Standard of Excellence**. This excites and inspires the team. A commitment to excellence moves the team from good to great and builds lasting momentum.

Every leader has momentum. It can either be positive or negative. Positive momentum produces growth and advancement, whereas negative momentum leads to status quo and eventually death. Just as there are life lines of momentum, there are also momentum killers. Take the opposite of the five life lines listed above and what you get are five momentum killers:

- **No Clear Vision**. People will not put positive energy into something that does not give a clear picture of where it is going. The saying is that if you don't know where you are going, any road will do and you won't know when you get there. Vision keeps people restrained and controlled. The lack of vision causes unrestrained and uncontrolled people. When this is present momentum dies a quick death.
- **Bad and Cowardly Decisions**. Leadership is all about making decisions. The greater the leadership responsibility the greater the decisions. Bad and cowardly decisions start the blame and the second guessing game that always kills momentum. There are times when a leader never recovers from this.
- **Wrong People**. People are the greatest asset to a leader, however, momentum is almost impossible to build with the wrong people, especially when they are in key positions. They are like holes in the hull of a boat. There have been great companies, organizations, and churches that were strong and influential only to bring in the wrong people and the momentum they had was killed. Today, they are only a shell of what they once were.
- **No Wins Under Your Belt**. Discouragement and disillusionment sets in when there are no wins. The morale is very low. In sports, if a team is on a long term losing streak, momentum is zapped out of the program. Attendance at the game wanes and support for the program is virtually nonexistent.
- **Mediocrity**. People are not inspired or excited by average. Doing just enough to get by is a recipe for failure. When there is not a standard for excellence and the bar is set low, followers will not be excited to excel and reach for all that is possible. The leader will work

twice as hard for less than half of the possible results. Mediocrity is a major momentum killer.

Great leaders build momentum and avoid the things that kill momentum. The difference between great leaders and everyone else is that great leaders actively create momentum, while other leaders wait passively maintaining the status quo (they wait to see if momentum will come to them).

It has been said that momentum is like a locomotive, once it is moving, it can plow straight through a six-foot thick wall of concrete. That same locomotive sitting idle on the track, however, can be held motionless by the tiniest four-inch block sitting on the track in front of it. Momentum can be the difference between winning and losing.

24

Networking

"If you're not networking, you're not working."
—Denis Waitley

"The way of the world is meeting people through other people."
—Robert Kerrigan

"More business decisions occur over lunch and dinner than at any other time, yet no MBA courses are given on the subject."
—Peter Drucker

"Position yourself as a center of influence - the one who knows the movers and shakers. People will respond to that, and you'll soon become what you project."
—Bob Burg

Networking is the practice of meeting other people involved in the same kind of work. Effective networkers share information and support each other. In leadership, networking is developing mutually beneficial relationships with other leaders in your field and other fields. It allows leaders to touch other leaders for the purposes of receiving information, resources, and training to which they would otherwise not have access. Networking is a powerful tool for leaders. It helps them build a rapport with other leaders from whom they can glean information that facilitates success in a chosen field of endeavor.

Every leader must come to the realization that to achieve great levels of success, he cannot do it alone. There are doors the leader will need to go through in which he does not have the key, and there will be people he will need to meet with whom there is no present and/or apparent connection. The way to overcome these potential barriers is by networking. Within your networking circle, you will find someone who has the key to the door or they will know someone who knows someone with the key to the door you need to go through. Also, in that circle, there will be someone connected to the person who will know someone connected to the person you need to meet.

The six degrees of separation (also referred to as the "Human Web") says that it takes just six steps to link any two people on the planet. That means that you are only six people away from any person on the planet. Therefore, networking is invaluable to leaders. There is an old saying that, "It's not what you know, it's who you know." In today's interconnected society, this rings true for a leader. As a leader, you must understand that your talents, abilities, and experience will never take you anywhere if nobody knows you exist. If you are going to go anywhere in life and succeed as a leader, you have to be resourceful. Other leaders are a vast resource.

Networking takes time and effort and it can also be very exhausting, unless you are the personality type that enjoys meeting people and making contacts. You have to see networking as an investment with benefits that outweigh the costs. Everyone you meet, whether they are in leadership, business, education, etc., represents a potential networking opportunity. The person may not be relevant to you and your situation at the present time, but they may become relevant at some point in the future. Even if they never become relevant to you, they may become an important resource for one of your other contacts. As you use your network for important connections, you should also be a connector for others.

The key to networking is taking the initiative and sharpening your conversational skills. Here are some tips for successful networking:

- **Introduce Yourself**. If you are an introvert, this is difficult. However, it is the first step to networking. You cannot network with those who do not know you and they won't know you unless you introduce yourself to them. This can also be done by a colleague. You must talk to people. You must be intentional about meeting as many people as possible.
- **Make a Good Presentation**. You only get one chance to make a first impression, so make sure you make a good one. Present yourself in a very confident manner. People will remember you if you make a compelling impression on them. Let them know what you do and how it might profit them in the future.
- **Get Contact Information**. Ask them for a business card or write down their phone numbers, e-mail and web address information. This is the bread and butter

of networking. If you fail here, you can go no further with the contact.

- **Follow Up**. Within twenty-four to forty-eight hours of the initial meeting, you should follow up with an email acknowledging the meeting and that you look forward to future interactions with them. Following up is what seals the deal to many networking opportunities

- **Make Use of Social Media**. In the 21st century, the way to get connected is through social media. Facebook, Twitter, LinkedIn and Instagram are powerful means to getting connected and networking. A leader not using social media today is stuck in the dark ages. It's the world we now live in.

Networking is about building relationships that will be mutually beneficial to both parties in the future. A leader must take advantage of every networking opportunity. They exist all around, from eating lunch at the restaurant, to going to the kid's ball game, to worshipping at church on Sundays. Why is networking important? According to U.S. Department of Labor Statistics, seventy percent of all jobs are found through networking. Imagine how many other business or non-business opportunities are opened up through networking.

People who are successful in leadership or in business have made great use of opportunities to network. It does not matter how sharp, talented, or charismatic you might be, deficiencies still exist. There will still be doors you cannot get opened on your own. There will be places you cannot take yourself. You will need someone else to run interference for you. To be the best you can be and to reach your maximum potential, you must have access to the key people and the best resources. The only way to achieve the access to key people and the best resources is to be connected. How do you get connected? It's simple, you get connected through networking. You may ask, "What can networking do for me?" It can open a whole new world of possibilities.

25

Opposition

"One-fifth of the people are against everything all the time."

—Robert F. Kennedy

"How far would Moses have gone if he had taken a poll in Egypt?"

—Harry S. Truman

"Don't be afraid of opposition. Remember, a kite rises against, not with the wind."

—Hamilton Wright Mabie

"Great spirits have always encountered violent opposition from mediocre minds."

—Albert Einstein

Opposition is an attempt to check, restrain, or defeat something. It is the act of opposing or resisting something in which you disapprove or disagree. Every leader will at one time or another experience opposition, from within and without. Opposition is an inevitable reality of leadership. Since it is an inevitable reality, it behooves the leader to harness his skills of how to handle opposition, criticism, and resistance.

There are radically different temperaments that apply to handling opposition. There are the leaders who thrive on opposition; they are not intimidated by it all. It energizes them. It causes them to bring all of their skills, strategies and energy to the forefront. They see opposition as a challenge and an opportunity. This individual's challenge is ensuring they have the ability to focus all of their energy and skill on overcoming the opposing forces that are committed to defeating their objectives.

When the Chicago Bulls were making their run winning six NBA championships during the 1990's, their superstar Michael Jordan said that during the playoffs he would rather play on the road in the opposing teams' stadiums than at home in the United Center. His reasoning was that he was playing before nineteen thousand fans rooting against him; this made him and the team focus more on the job at hand. He said the opportunity to silence and take the life out of the opposing crowd stirred something up in him that allowed him to perform at his highest level. In other words, the greatest basketball player of all time thrived on opposition. During their run, the Bulls won three of the six championships on the opponent's home courts. Also, during their run, their record on the road during the NBA Finals was 12 wins and 6 loses which is a .666 winning percentage. The great ones are not at all intimidated by opposition.

The second temperament belongs to leaders who hate opposition and seek appeasement at all costs. These leaders are peace seekers. They feel that if they give in a little or give ground, it will satisfy the opposition. In most cases it doesn't work out that way. The rule of thumb is that the opposition will not be satisfied with appeasement; they view appeasement as weakness and quickly assess the leader as incompetent and soft. This causes them to lose respect for the leader and they move in to kill his agenda. There is a time for appeasement, however, the leader must have the discernment to know when to appease and when not to.

Those who oppose you are only reacting to what they do not know or understand. The keys to handling opposition are simple. Here are five keys:

- **Expect Opposition.** When you expect opposition, it takes away the element of surprise. You are not taken aback when it comes. Know that great leaders with vision will always be opposed by those with mediocre thinking. Bishop T.D. Jakes says, "When opposition comes, give yourself a ten percent chance to be wrong, allow yourself a fifty percent likelihood of being betrayed, and a hundred percent commitment to survive it all." In other words, don't let opposition take you out.
- **Identify the Opposition.** Knowing the source of your opposition is part of the path to victory. Why? Because the source of the opposition will tell you more than the opposition itself. Once you identify the source of the opposition, you can begin to develop your strategy for confronting and dealing with the opposition.
- **Confront the Opposition.** Do not confront them in a hostile way but rather in a positive manner to find

out the basis for their opposition. Share your vision or plan with them and invite them to get on board. However, stand your ground and don't back up. This will also allow you to know the strength and resolve of the opposition.

- **Don't Personalize the Opposition**. Those who oppose you are in opposition to your vision, plans, and passion. They do not believe in the course you want to take. It is a lack of understanding. See it from that perspective and not as a personal opposition to you as a person. When you personalize it, you have stopped being the leader and you are now being led by the opinion of the opposition. Even if the opposition is personal, it's their problem not yours. You are still the leader.

- **Continue Your Vision Despite the Opposition**. In the midst of opposition, you must remain vision centered. Never sacrifice your vision for your critics. Do not let opposition distract you from your goal. An important secret to successful leadership is the ability to work through opposition. A leader must be resilient. Those who oppose will either get on board or be run over.

There is no such thing as an opposition free organization, church, or business. The plain truth is that if you lead, you will encounter opposition. You will never experience greatness or high levels of success until you learn how to handle opposition. Margaret Thatcher said it best when she said, "If it is once again one against forty-eight, then I am very sorry for the forty-eight."

26

Passion

"Nothing great in the world has ever been accomplished without passion."
—George Wilhelm Friedrich Hegel

"It is your passion that empowers you to be able to do the thing that you were created to do."
—T. D. Jakes

"One person with passion is better than forty people merely interested."
—E. M. Forster

"A genuine passion is like a mountain stream; it admits of no impediment; it cannot go backward; it must go forward."
—Christian Nestell Bovee

Passion is defined as any powerful or compelling emotion or feeling, an intense driving, or overmastering feeling or conviction. It is an abnormally strong desire or conviction toward a given thing. Passion is a very powerful force; it is an intangible that all truly great leaders have. Leadership experts have long concluded that influence is the engine that drives leadership. If influence is the engine that powers leadership, passion is the fuel that powers the engine.

Passion is crucial to becoming a great leader. As a matter of fact, without passion you have a zero chance of becoming a great leader. When you look at great leaders like Mahatma Gandhi, Martin Luther King, Jr., John F. Kennedy and Nelson Mandela, you will see that the common bond they all possessed is passion. I cannot name any great leaders that did not have passion.

Passion must not be directionless. It must be directed in a given area or towards a given thing, assignment, or goal. The great leaders have directed their passion to something that excites them. It is focused around a goal or an objective that they want to achieve. It is a part of the very fiber of their being. It goes to sleep with them at night and wakes up with them in the morning. Their passion is so intense that it cuts through obstacles, opposition, and negativity. There is nothing stronger than a leader with focused vision, direction, and the passion to get him there. A leader with passion will light the fire in the belly of those following and cause them to connect with his vision. The reason for this is that passion is contagious.

When a leader does not have passion, it is very difficult to inspire commitment from the followers. Barack Obama, the first African-American President of the United States, inspired the nation with his passion for change during his presidential campaign. So passionate was he about change, that in every speech and television advertisement it was the theme. It was not long before change went from being a campaign slogan to a national movement. His passion for change spread to millions of people of all races until the masses were crying out for change. From the primaries to the general election, there was nothing the opposition could do to stop this crusade that was moving like an out-of-control avalanche.

On Election Day in 2008, the change movement came full circle when America voted overwhelmingly for change... and history was made. But the genesis of the entire movement was the passion for change and the vision of change in Barack Obama. He never lost that passion throughout the two-year campaign. His passion caused people to connect with him and the campaign. Blacks and Whites, Asians and Hispanics, Democrats and Republicans, Independents and new voters were all drawn in by the passion that Obama possessed towards his cause. Passion caused people to lay aside their differences and come together for a common cause. When you look at the lives of great leaders, you will see that they all possess the five C's of passion:

- **Cause**. There must be something compelling for you to be passionate about. The cause becomes the foundation for your passion. Some have called it a sense of destiny, a hill to climb, a mountain to conquer or a continent to cross. It is something in which to give yourself. Where there is no cause, there is no passion.
- **Commitment**. Whatever the cause, your commitment to it will fuel your passion. It is the driving force behind your passion. You will never be passionate about what you are not committed. Commitment keeps you going

when others have long quit. It keeps you going even when you feel tired and weary.

- **Challenge**. Great leaders are passionate about things that challenge them. They commit themselves to causes that are bigger than them. The challenge will demand that a leader's greatest gifts and talents emerge. There is a David down on the inside of every great leader looking and waiting for Goliath to challenge him. They live for those moments. They understand that greatness arises out of challenges.

- **Chance**. Taking risks is an important part of living with passion. Leaders who are passionate about a cause embrace risk taking. They understand that nothing great can be achieved without risk. Some of the greatest achievements that leaders have achieved came as a result of taking a chance. These leaders are not reckless or presumptuous, but neither are they afraid to take a chance or a great risk. Their risks are calculated and well thought out. They live kind of close to the edge.

- **Confidence**. When you have passion about something, it breeds confidence. Passionate leaders have a very high degree of confidence in themselves and their abilities. They are not timid or slothful. They are fearless initiators. They are so confident until it can almost come across as arrogance. However, it is not arrogance, they just believe in themselves. Muhammad Ali, the great boxing champion, said, "To be a great champion you must believe that you are the best. If you're not, pretend you are."

Passion is a beautiful thing to watch in the life of leaders. To see the intensity that drives them is like a magnet that draws you to them. Passionate leaders are never satisfied with the status quo in themselves or in their organization. They are always seeking to learn more, looking for ways to reinvent themselves, and exploring new things and new methods of achieving their objectives. Leaders with passion are the ones who make things happen that bring change to the world.

27

Priorities

"Don't tell me where your priorities are. Show me where you spend your money and I'll tell you what they are."

—James W. Frick

"The key is not to prioritize what's on your schedule, but to schedule your priorities."

—Stephen R. Covey

"Decide what you want, decide what you are willing to exchange for it. Establish your priorities and go to work."

—H. L. Hunt

"Success is only another form of failure if we forget what our priorities should be."

—Harry Lloyd

Priorities are defined as something given or meriting attention that supersedes competing alternatives. A leader will always have things competing for his time and energy. Therefore, it is imperative that a leader develop the skill of prioritizing those things.

A major difference between effective leaders and ineffective leaders is how they prioritize their work and time. Effective leaders are focused on what is important. They give their skills and energy to the things that are the most productive to them and their organizations. They have disciplined themselves not to get drawn into trivial and menial tasks that do not bring much productivity. On the contrary, ineffective leaders are not very focused at all; they live from crisis to crisis. This is because they are always getting drawn into the non-important things that drain their time, while the truly important things go unchecked. When important things go unchecked, they become a crisis. Ineffective leaders lack the discipline to say no to the things to which they need to say no.

The Pareto principle is a good tool that a leader can use to assist him in the area of prioritizing. The Pareto Principle was named after the Italian economist Vilfredo Pareto, who observed that eighty percent of property in Italy was owned by twenty percent of the Italian population. It is generally called the 80/20 Rule and is also called "The Vital Few and Trivial Many Rule." The Pareto Principle states that eighty percent of the results from any series of actions are caused by only twenty percent of the actions. This means that most of the results in any situation are determined by a small number of causes. The observation of the Pareto Principle is that most things in life are not distributed evenly. It states that twenty percent of our priorities will give us eighty percent of our production if we spend our time, energy, money, and personnel on the top twenty percent of our priorities. Here are some examples of how this principle works:

- **Time**. Twenty percent of our time produces eighty percent of the results.
- **People**. Twenty percent of people take up eighty percent of our time.
- **Reading**. Twenty percent of the book contains eighty percent of the content.
- **Job**. Twenty percent of the work gives us eighty percent of our satisfaction.
- **Church**. Twenty percent of the people give eighty percent of the money.
- **Work**. Twenty percent of the people will do eighty percent of the work.
- **Products**. Twenty percent of the products bring eighty percent of the profits.
- **Picnic**. Twenty percent of the people will eat eighty percent of the food.

A leader must determine which of his priorities represent the top twenty percent and spend the majority (eighty percent) of his time and energy on these priorities. A leader will find that a consistent application of this rule will lead to significant improvement in productivity. While this rule is not an absolute, it can be used by leaders as a guide and reference point to determine whether or not they are truly focusing on the twenty percent which are the Vital Few, or the eighty percent which represent the Trivial Many.

The reverse of the Pareto Principle is that if leaders spend the majority of their time on those things that do not yield a return, or with the wrong people, they will not be effective. This is the trap that many ineffective leaders are snared into. A very effective tool to help leaders avoid this trap and set their priorities is the A-B-C-D-E method:

- **A**. Very important; must do; severe negative consequences if not completed.
- **B**. Important; should do; but not as important as my 'A' tasks, and only minor negative consequences if not completed.
- **C**. Nice to do; but not as important as 'A' or 'B,' and no negative consequences for not completing.
- **D**. Delegate, or assign to someone else who can do the task in their place.
- **E**. Eliminate, whenever possible.[20]

When leaders apply the A-B-C-D-E method, they can very easily sort out what is important and what is unimportant. This will allow them to focus their time, energy and attention on the things that are essential for them to do. Learning to manage priorities is another key to effective leadership. Effective leaders have developed the practice of not allowing life's demands and daily pressures to control their schedule or priorities. They plan their work and work their plan. This allows them to be proactive in their approach to leadership, as opposed to the alternative where the leader's practice is always reacting to urgent demands and crisis situations. Leaders who are successful at prioritizing their work see greater productivity in their work and experience greater satisfaction in their lives.

28

Risk

"Don't be afraid to go out on a limb. That's where the fruit is."
—H. Jackson Browne

"Yes, risk taking is inherently failure-prone. Otherwise, it would be called sure-thing-taking."
—Tim McMahon

"Only those who dare to fail greatly can ever achieve greatly."
—Robert F. Kennedy

"Only those who will risk going too far can possibly find out how far one can go."
—T. S. Eliot

Risk means taking chances in the hope of favorable outcomes. The outcome of the risk is not guaranteed, but it is a chance the leader feels must be made for the best benefit of the organization. Leadership requires some risk taking. Every leader would love for the path forward to be totally clear to them, but the reality is that many times when the endeavor to move forward is before the leader, the path is foggy and uncertain. However, to take the organization to the next level of growth and productivity or to achieve their own life goals and aspirations, they must be willing to take a risk.

Some of the greatest achievements in leadership and in business have come at the expense of someone taking risks. Those who have changed the world or who have had a great impact on world events were those who put it all on the line by taking a risk. Bill Gates and Paul Allen both took a risk and dropped out of college (Bill Gates – Harvard and Paul Allen – Washington State) to be co-founders of Microsoft. At the time, their risk looked foolish, but forty years later their company has changed the world and has made them two of the wealthiest men in the world. Michael Dell started a computer company called *PCs Limited* while attending the University of Texas at Austin. The company became successful enough that Dell took a risk and dropped out of school to operate it. The company eventually became Dell, Inc., with revenues of $57.4 billion in 2007. In 2006, Dell and his wife gave a $50 million grant to the university he attended, but from which he never graduated.

Risk taking does not mean that a leader should be reckless and make risky decisions without sound thought and strategic planning. Leaders should take calculated risks that have been given thoughtful consideration and for which the potential costs and potential benefits have been weighed and considered. Although risk taking is not blind chance and recklessness, it requires courage, overcoming the fear of failure, and the ability to analyze. The leader must be willing to possibly fail and get up and try again. Leaders must not live trying to avoid risks. Being overly cautious will cost the leader time and resources. A certain degree of risk is inevitable and unavoidable.

Risk taking leaders are those who see opportunities, rather than risks. These leaders are very confident and think on a different level. Therefore, they spot opportunity where others see overwhelming risks. Here are some points to consider when taking risks:

- **Establish Boundaries**. This determines the limits that you will not go beyond and places conditions on the risks you take. This is for the protection of the leader and the organization. The violation of this point has been the death of many companies and thus the leadership of the company.
- **Do Not Overanalyze.** Leaders have a tendency to suffer from paralysis of analysis. They spend so much time fretting about consequences and possible missteps that the plan gets stuck at the terminal and never gets on the runway for takeoff. It's prudent to analyze, just don't overanalyze.
- **Do Not Go Solo**. Use the wisdom of other great minds when making the decision to take a major risk. In the multitude of counsel, there is safety. When others are involved, they can spot potential blind spots that the leader did not detect. Having others involved also creates checks and balances.
- **Take The Leap**. After all the due diligence is done, the detailed planning completed, and all things have been considered, take the risk! There is nothing left to do but

to go for it. It may be a leap of faith, but that's what risk is. Believing that it will work, but having no guarantees.

• **Accept Responsibility.** If things go bad, don't pass the buck. Accept the responsibility and determine what went wrong while making the necessary adjustments. Know the consequences of a failed risk, be willing to accept the responsibility and live with the results.

• **Do Not Be A Martyr.** Don't kill the organization at the expense of trying to make the risks you took work. Know when to fold them. There are times when it's a greater risk to stay in a risk too long. A leader must have the courage to pull the plug and salvage what he can rather than continue on a Titanic course.

When it comes to risk taking, there are two kinds of leaders—those who do and those who do not. When contemplating taking a risk, a leader must ask the question, "Is this the right risk to take?" It is a failure of leadership not to take it, providing it is the right risk to take. Risk taking is necessary because without it leaders would not try anything new or innovative and there would not be much progress made. Jimmy Johnson, the former coach of the Dallas Cowboys, once asked, "Do you want to be safe and good, or do you want to take a chance and be great?" Leaders accomplish more by taking risks than by playing it safe.

29

Skill

"Skill and confidence are an unconquered army."
—George Hubert

"Few things are impossible to diligence and skill. Great works are performed not by strength, but perseverance."
—Samuel Johnson

"Wisdom is knowing what to do next, skill is knowing how to do it, and virtue is doing it."
—David Starr Jordan

"A winner is someone who recognizes his God-given talents, works his tail off to develop them into skills and uses these skills to accomplish his goals."
—Larry Bird

Skill is the learned capacity to carry out pre-determined results often with a minimum outlay of time, energy, or both. It is also the ability coming from one's knowledge, practice, and aptitude to do something well. Every leader has been gifted from God with a specific skill or set of skills. A leader must identify his skill or skill set and develop it to perform at maximum potential. All good leaders are equipped with a set of skills, but the great leaders have one or two skills that they have developed and totally maximized. It is what has taken them to the top in their respective fields. If you study the really great leaders, you will find that it is a specific skill that they have perfected to such a degree that it has become second nature to them.

There is a tendency sometimes for leaders to want to be good at everything. You really find this trait in poor and ineffective leaders. They spend so much of their time trying to be a jack of all trades that they never come to master the abilities in which they may really be good. This is not to say that a leader can't be good at several things. The point is that of all the things that a leader is good at, there will be one or two that truly dominate. Those are the ones to which he must apply eighty percent of his time. One of the great tragedies of leadership is to see a leader trying to function in an area in which he is not skilled.

In the arena of sports, Michael Jordan had a skill to play basketball. He developed that skill to the degree that he became the greatest basketball player of all time. However, when he attempted to play professional baseball, it was not a pretty sight. It was agonizing watching him try to hit major league pitching, especially the curve balls. Your skill is your strength. Basketball was his strength. When he attempted to play baseball, he moved away from his strength. Leaders do it all the time. In looking for a new challenge, they stray away from their strengths, which are their true skills. The overwhelming majority of these ventures end in failure like Jordan's baseball experiment. It takes a disciplined leader to stay in the lane where he is truly skilled. A leader's skills will come in two categories:

- **Natural Skills**. These are the skills that a leader possesses naturally. The leader was born with these skills and they develop naturally as he grows and matures. They can also be called natural abilities.
- **Acquired Skills**. These are skills that the leaders did not possess naturally, but that were learned through education/schooling, training seminars, mentoring, coaching, etc.

When combined, these two sets of skills become the single skill set of a leader. Every leader has a skill set. It is imperative that leaders identify their skill set and apply these strengths to their leadership responsibilities. When it comes to the skill set, leaders will do well by applying the Pareto Principle (aka "The 80/20 Rule") to their skills. Spend eighty percent of your time on the top twenty percent of your skill strengths and spend twenty percent on the remaining eighty percent. If, according to Pareto, the top twenty percent will give you eighty percent of your result, it's a no brainer where leaders should direct the majority of their time and attention when it comes to skill development.

The nature of a leader's role in leading will demand he utilize some level of skill in leading the organization. Some of the areas that a leader must develop and display skill in are:

- **Problem Solving**. Every organization will have its share of problems and problem people, so the leader had better get good at problem solving. This is a required skill of leaders.

- **Vision Casting**. The leader has to think, act, and communicate the vision. Everything the leader does should embody his commitment to the vision. This skill is where a leader motivates and inspires the followers to action.

- **Delegating**. The great leaders have mastered the art of getting things done through other people. This keeps the leader freed up to deal with the things that he is required to handle and not get bogged down in unimportant tasks.

- **Goal Setting**. This gives the people and the organization something in which to strive. Working toward achieving the goal is what keeps them coming back to work every day.

- **Motivating**. The ability to get people up and to keep them up is a skill that is invaluable to a leader. This is a common trait among all great athletic coaches. It takes skill to know the right buttons to push to get great athletes to perform at their maximum level. Leaders must also know the right buttons to push.

- **Creative Thinking**. The 21st century has put a demand on leaders to think outside the box. They must create new ways to perform their tasks more efficiently without compromising their core values.

- **Team Building**. Building alliances through teams is the way things are done in the culture of the 21st century. The day of the lone ranger has passed. You cannot do it alone. Bring skilled, talented and gifted people alongside you to accomplish the organization's objectives.

When I played slow pitch softball, teams would normally put their weakest skilled defensive player in right field. The reason for this is that most batters are right handed and, therefore, it is not natural for them to hit to right field. In fact, teams would put him there because they felt he could do minimal damage out there. When we realized that our opponent had a weakness in right field, we would purposely hit toward right field over and over again thus exposing their weakness. We would say to our opponent, "You can't hide him." The same is true in leadership. There is no substitute for skill, either you have it or you don't. A leader without skill cannot be hidden; he will get exposed because the organization or company will fizzle under his leadership.

30

Strategy

"There is nothing so useless as doing efficiently that which should not be done at all."

—Peter Drucker

"The essence of strategy is choosing what not to do."

—Michael Porter

"Achieve success in any area of life by identifying the optimum strategies and repeating them until they become habits."

—Charles J. Givens

"There is always a better strategy than the one you have; you just haven't thought of it yet."

—Sir Brian Pitman

Strategy is the means by which objectives are pursued and obtained over time. It is a plan of action designed to achieve a particular goal. The word strategy has military connotations because it derives from the Greek word for general. Strategy is different than tactics. In military terms, tactics is concerned with the conduct of an engagement, while strategy is concerned with how different engagements are linked. In other words, how a battle is fought is a matter of tactic; the terms under which it is fought and whether it should be fought at all are matters of strategy.[21]

In terms of a church, the strategy encompasses the vision. In other words, the strategy would be what we want to do, what the end game will be, or how the church will look at the end of the day when the vision is fulfilled. The tactics would be the ministries and programs put in place to accomplish the vision. Every leader of a company, organization, church, or business is involved in strategizing. The leader must be a strategic thinker. The leader, as strategist, is responsible for the vision, direction, growth, and success of the organization. Leaders must also know that strategy involves options.

The strategy should specify what actions would be taken in different phases of the organization's growth and development. For example, there are problems and issues that you will face at level two that you did not face at level one. So the strategic option is that when problem A occurs, one must take option B. When you take a panoramic view of strategy, you discover the things that strategy is concerned with:

- **Direction**. Where are we going? Do we have it written clearly in our organizational documents? The leader has the responsibility to make sure that everyone in the leadership team and the organization at large knows the direction that the organization is headed. This cannot be left to chance; it has to be drilled and drilled until it is a normal part of everyone's thinking.

- **Resources**. What resources (finances, facilities, and skilled people) will we need to achieve our objectives? The leader, with his leadership core, must answer this question and determine how they will generate finances, upgrade the facilities, and recruit the skilled people needed.
- **Target**. Who is our target audience that we are trying to reach? Are we structured to reach them? Do we relate to and understand the thinking of our target audience? What are their needs? Do our services and products address their needs? The development of strategy must answer these questions.
- **Advantage**. How can we perform better than our competition? Why should people pass on the others to come to us? The strategy must highlight the organization's uniqueness which consists of the things that set your organization apart from all like organizations. Build on your strengths and your uniqueness. You cannot be all things to all people.
- **Leadership**. What are the values and expectations of those who are leaders in the organization? What is the process for choosing leaders? Leaders should be expected to maintain impeccable character and integrity. They should lead by precept and example.

Leaders should make sure that their strategy is good and sensible. A bad strategy can be the downfall of a leader and the organization. A good example of a bad strategy is the one employed by the former leader and dictator of Iraq, Saddam

Hussein. He concocted a strategy to convince the world, especially the United States, that he had weapons of mass destruction in order to prevent an invasion.

The strategy was severely flawed on a couple of fronts. First, the strategy eventually encouraged the invasion he was trying to avoid. Second, he never told his generals that the weapons of mass destruction were an illusion and a fabrication of his imagination. The generals were expecting to use them against the Americans as they marched on Bagdad. In the end, bad strategy cost Saddam the war and ultimately his life.

The lessons that a leader learns from Saddam Hussein are that strategy must be based on reality and it should never be used as a diversionary mechanism. Also, a leader should never leave his leadership team in the dark concerning strategy whereby causing them to be functioning on flawed information.

In sports, the best coaches are the ones who are the best game strategists. The same is true in leadership. The best leaders are strategists. A leader must resemble a good chess player. In the game of chess, the good chess players are always strategizing. They are always three or four moves ahead of where the game is. If they are not, the match is already lost. If his thinking is only in the present (where the organization is), he is already out of the game.

Effective leaders are always strategizing and anticipating bumps in the road and preparing for the next move. Without a strategy, a leader may know where he wants to go but he will have no clue of how to get there. Strategy is the course a leader takes to get the organization where the vision says it should go. It is the journey to the desired destination. Strategy is non-existent without a destination. Strategy, then, exists only in relation to a goal, end or objective.

31

Thinking

"A man is but the product of his thoughts; what he thinks, he becomes."

—**Mahatma Gandhi**

"Your thoughts are the architects of your destiny."

—**David O. McKay**

"We are addicted to our thoughts. We cannot change anything, if we cannot change our thinking."

—**Santosh Kalwar**

"To think is easy. To act is difficult. To act as one thinks is the most difficult."

—**Johann Wolfgang von Goethe**

To think is to analyze, examine, sort through information, and form ideas and opinions in the mind. This allows for the performance of mental operations such as reasoning. The thinking process of a leader is of utmost importance. A leader's thought process is what sets the pace for the organization and develops the culture of the organization. A careful observation of highly successful companies or organizations will uncover the methods in which the leaders lead. The result of the leader's thoughts and behaviors will trickle down throughout the company and have a tremendous impact on the performance of the organization's associates.

A leader's success or failure is directly connected to his ability to think, as he is always thinking and strategizing. Good leaders are good thinkers, great leaders are great thinkers and poor leaders are poor thinkers. Leaders fall into one of two categories relative to thinking; they either think inside the box or they think outside the box.

Thinking inside the box is using the normal route to a solution and it is usually the safest route. Thinking inside the box means accepting the status quo. A perfect example of this is in 1899 when Charles H. Duell, Director of the U.S. Patent Office, said, "Everything that can be invented has been invented." In-the-box thinkers are skillful at killing ideas. They are masters of the creativity killer attitude such as "that'll never work" or "it's too risky."[22]

Thinking outside the box is taking a stand against the normal. Outside the box thinkers are open to new ways of looking at things. They are able to take risks and to look at things from a different perspective. Thinking outside the box does not mean designating the old way of doing things as wrong; it simply means not being afraid to try something that seems different. Leaders who are outside the box thinkers readily accept the fact that they will face ridicule from those who fail to embrace new perspectives.

Leaders see what others do not and that's what distinguishes them from followers. They bring the future into the present. The greatest difference between leaders and followers is how they think about things. Followers, many times, see and think about things from a narrow tunnel vision point of view. However, leaders have to see and think of things from a panoramic view. There are many things that leaders think about differently:

- **Leaders think differently about themselves.** They believe in themselves. They have the utmost confidence in their abilities. They are mentally and emotionally strong.

- **Leaders think differently about others.** They believe in those who are helping them. They are not threatened by them but support and encourage them. They want them to reach their goals and they will help them to reach their goals.

- **Leaders think differently about change.** They do not see change as the enemy, nor are they afraid of change. They embrace change and see it as the vehicle to get them to the next level. They understand that in order to make progress, change is necessary.

- **Leaders think differently about obstacles.** They view obstacles as opportunities. They are not deterred by obstacles. They feel that obstacles cause the best in them to come forth.

- **Leaders think differently about commitment to the vision.** Their commitment is not something that is part-time. Their commitment to the vision is twenty-four seven. It lives with them and can be seen in all they do. Their commitment is neither based on conditions nor emotions. It is based on a decision they have made, therefore, their commitment is rock solid.

- **Leaders think differently about what it is possible to accomplish**. They believe that they can accomplish great things. They believe that if they can get the team unified and committed, nothing can stop them from accomplishing anything in which they set their minds.
- **Leaders think differently about life**. They believe that they have been put on this earth for a purpose. They live their lives with a sense of purpose and destiny in mind. Therefore, every decision they make and every action they take is done in view of purpose and destiny. They live life as though they are on assignment. Carrying out the assignment creates fulfillment for them.

It has been said that great thinking and great leadership go hand-in-hand. When you find a great leader, you have come across great thinking. Roger Martin conducted interviews with fifty effective leaders and discovered that they are integrative thinkers, meaning that they can hold in their heads two opposing ideas at once and come up with a new idea that contains elements of each, but that is superior to both.[23]

Leaders should be positive thinkers. This does not mean that they take leave of reality, it means that even when facing the most dismal facts, they remain positive in negative situations. They think win-win rather than win-lose. Leaders understand that both positive and negative thinking are contagious and they are both amplified when coming from the leader. Therefore, in order to have the greatest impact upon those they lead, they must exhibit positive thinking.

Leaders are always looking for things to stimulate their minds to think, not just to learn new things but to act in new ways. Leaders see and think about every situation from a leadership perspective. Their thought processes will not allow them to accept mediocrity or defeat. They think that they can win any battle and overcome every obstacle. What do the great leaders think? They think win and not lose. They can accept occasional losses, but they never get comfortable with them. To them, winning is everything and losing is not an option.

32

Trust

"To be trusted is a greater compliment than being loved."

—George MacDonald

"Whoever is careless with the truth in small matters cannot be trusted with important matters."

—Albert Einstein

"Trust is the easiest thing in the world to lose, and the hardest thing in the world to get back."

—R. Williams

"The glue that holds all relationships together, including the relationship between the leader and the led, is trust and trust is based on integrity."

—Brian Tracy

The Merriam-Webster's Online Dictionary defines trust as assured reliance on the character, ability, strength, or truth of someone or something; one in which confidence is placed. In leadership, trust is the confidence and reliance that those following have placed in the leader's ability to lead. Trust is the foundation of leadership. The entire essence of leadership is built upon a foundation of trust. If the foundation of trust crumbles, the leader's ability to lead effectively will crumble also.

Trust has always been vital to leadership and without trust, effective leadership is not possible. When a leader loses the trust of his followers, he loses the capacity to influence them, and when you cannot influence them, they will not follow you. So the simple fact is that if you lose the trust of your followers and you lose your ability to lead them, it is highly unlikely you will be able to influence. When a leader loses trust, he also opens up Pandora's Box within the organization. He opens himself up to disorganization, division, and even betrayal.

Once a leader is given trust, it is imperative that he make every attempt to maintain that trust. Many articles have been written about how to regain trust and many of them offer good insight on rebuilding trust. However, the best scenario is to never lose it. Commit yourself to maintaining trust and you won't have to worry about regaining it. An often-asked question is, "Is trust given or is it earned?" The answer is both. It is given and it is earned. A leader is given a certain level of trust with the position of leadership. I call this positional trust because it is the minimum amount of trust that comes with the position. This is the lowest level of trust that a leader can have (other than not having any trust). All leaders start at this level. At this level, your influence is minimal. You do not have room for errors, misjudgments, mistakes, or moral failures at this level. Missteps can be fatal to a leader at this level because the trust gauge is very near empty.

A leader can also earn trust from those he is leading. I call this earned trust. He earns trust by the things he does for his followers and the organization. Positional trust is limited, but earned trust has no limits. There is no limit to how much trust a leader can earn. A high level of earned trust takes time and consistency to build. A perfect example of someone who has built up a high level of earned trust is Billy Graham. He is not only respected and trusted by the Christian community, but the secular world respects and trusts him highly also. He has never been involved in any scandal, never been accused of any financial impropriety and he does not live a lavish lifestyle. He always ranks at the top of polls on who is the most trusted Christian leader. Presidents, world leaders, business leaders and the like have all sought out his services at one time or another because of the level of trust he has earned.

The more earned trust a leader has, the more influence and goodwill he has. The goodwill he has built allows room for errors and missteps without fatality. Character is very important to building up earned trust. If trust is the foundation of leadership, character is the foundation of trust. You will not earn trust if your character is flawed. Followers will forgive occasional honest mistakes due to lack of competence, but they will not tolerate flaws in character. How is trust earned? There are several ways:

- **Be a person of good character.** This is the surest and quickest way to gain people's trust. Having character denotes that you know the right things and you do the right things. It is what you do when no one is watching. It means that there is not a gap between what you say and what you do.

- **Honor your word**. People will trust you when they see that your word is your bond. In order for a leader to gain trust, he must be believable. If a leader's word is no good, the leader is no good. The followers need to know that the leader's word is as sure as the sun rising in the morning.
- **Maintain impeccable integrity**. The whole fabric of trust erodes when a leader's integrity is compromised. Trust is automatic when people know that the leader is a person of integrity. A leader without integrity has no chance of gaining trust from people.
- **Do things right and proper**. Don't take short cuts; they will only short circuit people's trust in you. The leader must practice ethical behavior in order to gain and maintain the trust of his followers. A leader should exhibit morals in all of his dealings.
- **Love the people you lead**. When people feel that the leader genuinely loves them, they will trust him, follow him, and obey him. The saying is, "People don't care how much you know until they know how much you care." Trust is the trade off a leader gets for loving the people he leads.

Trust is the currency of leadership and is a powerful force for a leader to have. When a leader has it, he is rich; when he doesn't, he is poor. When properly utilized, trust can make a leader unstoppable because the people are with him heart and soul. When misused, it can do damage that is irreparable, unforgettable, and leaves a trail of indescribable bitterness. A leader should always remember that the most precious thing that his followers can give him is their trust. He should honor their trust and most of all be true to their trust.

33

Values

"Personal leadership is the process of keeping your vision and values before you and aligning your life to be congruent with them."
—Stephen Covey

"It's not hard to make decisions when you know what your values are."
—Roy Disney

"Open your arms to change, but don't let go of your values."
—Dalai Lama

"Try not to become a man of success, but rather try to become a man of value."
—Albert Einstein

Values are deeply held beliefs about what is good, right, and appropriate. Values represent a philosophy that is really meaningful to the leader. They are those things that really matter to each of us; the ideas and beliefs we hold as special. Every leader possesses a personal code of values that are the principles or qualities that are fundamentally important to him. These values represent his convictions, his beliefs, and his ethics.

The formulation of a leader's values begin during the leader's childhood. They are based upon his observation and the teachings of his parents and other influential people in his life such as his pastor, teachers, or relatives. A leader's values are not just surface ideologies he thinks about every now and then. They are deeply rooted within him and at the very core of his being. They are like the stars in the galaxy, fixed in place and a constant factor within its realm. Neither time, culture, nor circumstances change a leader's values. They are the essence of who the leader is. When you observe good and successful leaders, the one common denominator is that they all live in agreement with their values. They do this because they understand that their values impact the organization. In every decision they make, their values come into play, whether those decisions are personnel decisions, financial decisions, or directional decisions. They are not made separately from their values.

It is during times of crisis, turmoil, and change that a leader's values are truly tested. In these situations, there is enormous pressure for a leader to abandon his values and make decisions that are in conflict with them. However, a values driven leader will always stay true to his values no matter what the cost. One of the most dissatisfying and unfulfilling things a leader can do is live in conflict with his values. There is long list of leaders who are living in the frustration that comes when they do things that are diametrically opposed to their values.

A leader is expected to lead by example. One of the most powerful ways that a leader can lead by example is to uncompromisingly live his values. A leader must live them visibly before those whom he leads so they can see them and be impacted by them. When a leader lives and implements his values, an energy is released into the organization that builds the framework for success in the company and with everyone in the organization.

What values should a leader possess? That depends upon the leader. Below are two lists of values. The first is a set of values that a leader might bring to the organization. The second is a common set of personal values that a leader might possess. Neither list is conclusive; they are just the framework from which to start.

List 1

- **Teamwork**. We work together as a team. The team is more important than any single individual.
- **Accountability**. All team members are responsible for the completion of tasks, assignments and projects.
- **Loyalty**. We are loyal and committed to the organization, the leadership, and the team members.
- **Integrity**. We will operate honestly and honorably. We will not say one thing and do another thing.
- **Innovation**. We will venture into new and different opportunities. We will not be trapped in the status quo.
- **Unity**. We will all be on the same page. There is room for only one vision in an organization.

- **People Development**. We are committed to helping you to be the best you can be and to reach your goals. We will develop the leader within you.

List 2

Achievement	Faith	Personal Growth
Commitment	Family	Reliability
Communication	Flexibility	Respect For Others
Competence	Fun	Service (to others)
Creativity	Generosity	Simplicity
Decisiveness	Honesty	Stability
Excellence	Leadership	Timeliness

Every leader is inspired to lead in a certain way. That inspiration is determined by the values that he has subscribed to and embraced. Without values, a leader would be like a robot, driven here and there by the unexpected changes of life and business. The leader would be forced to lead solely by his emotions and urges. Since leadership begins with the leader, so must the values of the organization begin with and be first demonstrated by the leader.

34

Vision

"When you have vision it affects your attitude. Your attitude is optimistic rather than pessimistic."
—Charles R. Swindoll

"Having a vision for your life allows you to live out of hope, rather than out of your fears."
—Stedman Graham

"Leadership is the capacity to translate vision to reality."
—Warren Bennis

"Great leaders communicate a vision that captures the imagination and fires the hearts and minds of those around them."
—Joseph B. Wirthlin

A vision is a clear mental picture of what a leader or an organization would like to achieve or accomplish in the mid-term or long-term future. It is intended to serve as a clear guide for choosing current and future courses of action. Vision is seeing the invisible and making it visible. It is dreaming the possible dream. However, for a leader, vision is not just a dream; it is a reality that has yet to come into existence. Leaders with vision are often referred to as visionaries. Vision is a compelling force that will compel the leader to tireless action to make the dream a reality. A leader with vision has the ability to see into the future without being far-sighted and remain rooted in the present without being near-sighted.[24]

The thing that separates a leader from everyone else is that the leader has vision. He has looked out over the horizon and seen where he wants to go and where he wants to take the organization. A leader with vision is a beautiful thing to behold. His whole life and being is consumed by the vision in his heart. He charts the course of the organization and his life by the vision in his heart.

The communication of vision by a leader to his followers inspires them to action. Vision has a way of awakening the dead, motivating the unmotivated, giving needed fuel to those running on empty, and giving direction to the directionless. Vision is powerful relative to its effect on people in the organization. Burt Nanus, a well know expert on leadership, lists a number of things that vision can accomplish for the organization:

- **It attracts commitment and energizes people.** When people can see that the organization is committed to a vision, it increases the commitment of people to work toward achieving that vision.

- **It creates meaning in workers' lives**. A vision allows people to feel like they are part of a greater whole, and hence, provides meaning for their work.
- **It establishes a standard of excellence**. A vision serves a very important function in establishing a standard of excellence.
- **It bridges the present and the future**. The right vision takes the organization out of the present and focuses it on the future. It is easy to get caught up in the crises of the day and to lose sight of where you were heading. A good vision can orient you on the future, and provide positive direction.[25]

Vision can be so compelling that only a leader knows what to do with it. Only a leader can marshal the resources necessary to bring life to the vision. Visionaries are always seeking to learn. They live in a continuous learning posture. They are not interested in who gets credit as much as they are in the vision emerging and producing the desired end result. They see difficult times as maturing opportunities that will ultimately result in breaking through to new heights and new levels.

Visionaries are not afraid of risk. As a matter of fact, they justify the risk by asserting that if there is not risk, there will be no change. If there is no change, progress will be stymied. Vision is also the glue that binds individuals into a group with a common goal. When followers understand the leader's vision, they can understand where the organization is going and what they are trying to accomplish. A vision should excite people by appealing to that side of them that wants to do something meaningful and accomplish something great. To some in the organization, the vision might seem overwhelming and beyond the realm of accomplishment. This has a way of draining faith and energy. The leader must be able to see through the uncertainty, reinforce the people's courage and keep them in pursuit of the vision. This is why leadership is critical to vision. A leader has a way of keeping things in perspective so that the vision is not sabotaged. To sum it up, a leader's vision is his marching orders. It helps him to say yes to some things and no to other things. Anything that is in line with his vision, his response is yes; anything that is not in line with his vision, his response is no. Without his marching orders, he wanders helplessly and aimlessly. The following list shows what a leader without a vision is like:

- **A cow loose in the pasture**. Just grazing.
- **A glacier**. Fascinating to observe, but going nowhere fast.
- **A snake**. Ill-focused, spineless and attracted to whatever is hot.
- **A movie set**. Merely a façade.
- **A flashlight without batteries**. Willing but powerless.
- **A wedding without a bride**. Missing an essential element.
- **A cadaver**. Stiff, predictable and lacking a discernible heartbeat.
- **A car without gasoline**. Capable of forward movement, but lacking the necessary fuel.
- **A symphony without a score**. Lots of talent, but no direction.[26]

The leader must communicate the vision tirelessly, fearlessly and with great conviction. If a leader fails in this regard, the vision has a very slim chance of seizing the followers. Vision is designed to stir people to action. The importance of vision cannot be understated. Vision is the life blood of leadership. It is impossible to lead effectively without a vision. Helen Keller, who overcame the misfortune of being blind and deaf to become one of the 20th century's leading humanitarians, summed it up when she said, "The only thing worse than being blind is having sight but no vision." It is even sadder when a leader doesn't have vision.

35

Wisdom

"God grant me the serenity to accept the things that I cannot change, courage to change the things I can, and wisdom to know the difference."
—Reinhold Niebuhr

"Wise men speak because they have something to say; fools because they have to say something."
—Plato

"Wisdom is knowing what to do next, skill is knowing how to do it, and virtue is doing it."
—David Starr Jordan

"How much better is it to get wisdom than gold, and to get understanding rather to be chosen than silver."
King Solomon (Proverbs 16:16)

P. Ronald Wilder

According to the Collins English Dictionary, wisdom is the ability to think and act using knowledge, common sense and insight. Wisdom is not something gained in an instant but wisdom is a process of continual learning. Leaders do not learn wisdom in a school classroom, but rather in the school of life where they live out their leadership in real life situations. They make decisions right and wrong that affect the lives of other people. From the consequences of those decisions, they gain wisdom. Leaders need wisdom to lead effectively and successfully. A leader who leads without wisdom is like a person driving an automobile while intoxicated; it is an accident waiting to happen. He is leading while impaired.

The book of Proverbs in the Bible identifies wisdom as the most important thing. *"Wisdom is the principal thing; therefore get wisdom: and with all thy getting get understanding. Exalt her, and she shall promote thee: she shall bring thee to honour, when thou dost embrace her."* (Proverbs 4:7-8, KJV). This means that "nothing" can compare with wisdom. Therefore it is supreme, well worth all the effort and cost involved in acquiring it.[27] If wisdom is this essential to everyday life, how much more essential is it in the life of a leader who is charged with the responsibility of leading people and making decisions for the organization? Wisdom has transformative power in that it can transform a good leader into a great leader while a poor leader can begin to use wisdom and be transformed into a good leader.

Many scholars regard King Solomon as the wisest man to ever live other than Jesus Christ. Solomon's forty year reign as king is considered to be the best of all the years in Israel's history. They were forty years of peace and prosperity. What made his leadership tenure so successful? The answer is wisdom. As he takes the reigns of leadership in Israel, the Lord appears to Solomon and said to him, "What do you want? Ask, and I will give it to you!"²⁸ Of all the things Solomon could have asked for he asked for wisdom. ⁹*"Give me an understanding heart so that I can govern your people well and know the difference between right and wrong. For who by himself is able to govern this great people of yours?"* ¹⁰ *The Lord was pleased that Solomon had asked for wisdom.* ¹¹ *So God replied, "Because you have asked for wisdom in governing my people with justice and have not asked for a long life or wealth or the death of your enemies—* ¹² *I will give you what you asked for! I will give you a wise and understanding heart such as no one else has had or ever will have!* ¹³ *And I will also give you what you did not ask for—riches and fame! No other king in all the world will be compared to you for the rest of your life!* (1 Kings 3:9-13, NLT).

The above passage of scripture shows how important it is for a leader to have wisdom. Wisdom to a leader means that he has the ability to discern and properly judge what is right and wrong. Wisdom gives a leader the insight to see what others cannot see. It allows him to penetrate beyond the surface of situations in order to ascertain the best course of action. Leadership requires making tough decisions and solving complex problems that do not have easy answers. This is where wisdom is critical to a leader. Wisdom allows a leader to ask the right questions and make the right observations in order to arrive at the correct conclusion and decision.

When the leader leads with wisdom, the people are led accurately and the organization flourishes. However, the acquisition of wisdom is not automatic in the life of a leader. It must be pursued in order to be attained. The quest for wisdom by a leader must be met with determination. The leader seeks wisdom with relentless resolve. There are keys to obtaining wisdom that a leader should embrace. They are:

- **Seek God for wisdom**. God is the source of wisdom, therefore, it behooves a leader to go to the source. *"The LORD by wisdom founded the earth, by understanding He established the heavens."* (Proverbs 3:19). *"But if any of you lacks wisdom, let him ask of God, who gives to all generously and without reproach, and it will be given to him."* (James 1:3).

- **Give heed to wise counsel.** The Bible says that in the multitude of counselors there is safety. The word safety can also be applied as wisdom. Wisdom can be found in wise counselors. The leader must listen and give heed to wisdom from those who are wise. *"And the counsel of Ahithophel, which he counselled in those days, was as if a man had enquired at the oracle of God: so was all the counsel of Ahithophel both with David and with Absalom."* (2 Samuel 16:23, KJV).

- **Associate with wise people.** The saying goes that association brings about assimilation. It means that you become the sum total of the people to which you associate. Make it a priority to associate with people who are wiser, smarter, and sharper than you, and it will have a direct, positive impact on you in the area of wisdom acquisition. *"He who walks with wise men will be wise, but the companion of fools will suffer harm."* (Proverbs 13:20).

- **Life experiences**. There is no greater teacher than the life experiences that we encounter. These experiences are both positive and negative. They are definite and unavoidable. A leader can acquire great amounts of wisdom by learning the lessons from these life experiences. Life is full of hills, valleys, curves, sharp turns, crevasses, and steep declines. In all of these, there are lessons, opportunities, and defining moments. "The difference between school and life? In school, you're taught a lesson and then given a test. In life, you're given a test that teaches you a lesson." (Tom Bodett)

• **Learn from others' mistakes.** Leaders before you have already traveled the road you are traveling or about to travel. Save yourself time, effort and energy by learning from their mistakes so you don't have to repeat them. Life is too short for you to have to figure everything out after you have made mistakes that could have been avoided by learning from others' mistakes. A wise man (leader) will learn from others' mistakes, but fools never learn.

Wisdom is therefore essential to a leader. Much is dependent upon the leader and his ability to lead effectively. Although there are other components that are needed for effective leadership such as vision, integrity, and skill, wisdom would also sit high in the hierarchy of the things needed for leadership success. Some of the reasons that leaders need wisdom are:

• **Leaders are required to make prudent decisions**. Their decisions sometimes will make or break the organization. Wisdom is needed to show them the way.

• **Leaders are required to solve problems and conflicts**. Sometimes there are no easy answers and there is no way to avoid casualties. Wisdom is needed to tread very sensitive ground.

• **Leaders are required to have insight.** They have to be able to see beyond the illusion, beyond the confusion, and beyond the distractions in order to shape strategy and direction. Wisdom is needed to make the dark light and the foggy clear.

- **Leaders are required to lead**. Leaders can delegate a lot of duties, but leading is one he cannot delegate. He alone must bear the burden of leadership. The buck must stop with him. Everything will rise or fall on him. With such a burden on his shoulders, wisdom is needed to be his constant companion, twenty four seven, three sixty five (24/7/365).

Leaders need wisdom to lead. When leaders fail to apply wisdom, the results can be disastrous. Wisdom is available to every leader. However, the leader must apply the desire, drive, and discipline needed to obtain wisdom. In sports, when a player is performing at a high level, it is said that he is at the top of his game. Wisdom keeps a leader at the top of his game.

Conclusion

Are leaders born or are leaders made? That question has been asked and debated for years with a variety of answers. There are people on both sides of the equation. This author believes that both sides are correct. Leaders are born and leaders are made. There are people born with the innate ability to lead. They have exhibited leadership qualities throughout their lives—from playing in the school yard straight through to adult life and into the leadership roles they are now fulfilling. I also believe that world changing leaders do not just accidently fall into leadership; they are born to lead, i.e., Martin Luther King, Jr., Mahatma Gandhi, Nelson Mandela, and the like. These leaders were not made into leaders; they were born leaders.

Then, there are those who learn and become leaders by personal development and there are those who accomplish this through reading, studying, observing other leaders, being mentored, and being coached. They may never reach world leadership status, but they can be effective and very good leaders in the company, organization, church, or business in which they lead.

The principles you have read in this book are designed to aid in your leadership development. As the leader, you are the key to your organization's success or failure. John Maxwell, often says that, "Everything rises and falls on leadership."[29] Based upon that statement, the success of any organization, business, company, church, etc., depends upon the leaders involved in it.

Leaders have to rise to and perform at high levels and maintain consistent and continued growth and development.

Now that you have read *The ABC's of Leadership*, you have received principles that will enhance your leadership development and assist you in performing at a higher level of leadership. Begin to practice and add to your life the things that you learned in this book. It may be a bit overwhelming to attempt to apply them all at once. If you have been in a leadership position for any period of time, you probably are already practicing some of these principles. It would be helpful to identify the most important principles that are lacking in your leadership style and work on those first, then continue to go down the list. You must remember that leadership development is not an event, it is a journey. It is my desire and hope that this book will be with you continually as you take your journey to becoming a great leader.

Endnotes

1   John Maxwell, The Winning Attitude (Nashville, TN: Thomas Nelson Publishers, 1993), 24.
2   Jim Collins, Good To Great, (New York, NY: HarperCollins Publishers, 2001), 39.
3   Lambert, Craig (March/April 2002), "Bobby Jones", Harvard Magazine.
4   J. Hampton Keathley, III, Marks of Maturity: Biblical Characteristics of a Christian Leader: The Pursuit of Excellence, http://www.bible.org/page.php?page_id=454.
5   Wikipedia, http://en.wikipedia.org/wiki/Failure
6   http://www.snopes.com/glurge/lincoln.asp
7   en.wikipedia.org/wiki/Fear
8   http://www.goal-setting-guide.com/smart-goals.html
9   Taken from John Maxwell, Thinking For A Change, (Warner Books), 12-13.
10 Rob Waldman, http://www.yourwingman.com/wing-blog/2012/03/14/the-price-of-integrity/
11 General Robert R. Folgeman, *The Leadership-Integrity Link*, (Concepts for Air Force Leadership)
12 Jim Collins, Good to Great, (New York, NY: HarperCollins Publishers, 2001), 41.
13 Noel Tichy & Warren Bennis, Judgment: How Winning Leaders Make Great Calls, (New York, NY: Penguin Group, 2007)
14 Rolston, Lynn and McNemey Denise, Article, Leading During Times of Crisis; Innovative Leader. May 2003
15 J. Robert Clinton, Leadership Perspectives, (Altadena, CA: Barnabas Publishers, 1993), 86-88.
16 Ken Blanchard, Article, Ignite, The online newsletter from The Ken Blanchard Companies, July 2004.
17 en.wikipedia.org/wiki/Bill Walsh (American football coach)
18 Holy Bible, King James Version, Matthew 10:8.

19   John Maxwell, Article, <u>Replacing Complacency</u>, www. maximumimpact.com, January 2006.

20   Brian Tracy, http://www.time-management-tools.com/articles/setting-priorities.htm

21   http://www.en.wikipedia/wiki/Strategy

22   Ed Bernacki, Article, <u>Exactly what is 'Thinking Outside the Box'?</u>, April 2002

23   Roger Martin, Article, <u>How Successful Leaders Think</u>, Harvard Business Review, June 2007

24   <u>Neil H. Snyder, Michelle Graves,</u> Business Horizons, Jan-Feb, 1994

25   Burt Nanus, Article, <u>Strategic Vision</u>, http://www.au.af.mil/au/awc/awcgate/ndu/strat-ldr-dm/pt4ch18.html

26   George Barna, <u>Turning Vision Into Action</u> (Regal Books, 1996).

27   Bible Knowledge Commentary, Page 913.

28   Holy Bible, <u>New Living Translation</u>, 1 Kings 3:5.

29   John Maxwell, <u>Developing The Leaders Around You</u> (Nashville: Thomas Nelson, Inc. Publishers, 1995), 6

About the Author

P. Ronald Wilder is the senior pastor of Covenant Church International, a nondenominational church located in Birmingham, Alabama. Pastor Wilder is a unique gift to the Body of Christ whose assignment is to raise leaders for the harvest and to expand the kingdom of God. He is a very passionate leader who is anointed and gifted by God to preach, teach, and expound the Word of God in a way that is easily grasped and applied in day-to-day life. Pastor Wilder is a graduate of SOUTHWESTERN CHRISTIAN UNIVERSITY located in Bethany, Oklahoma, where he received his Master's Degree in *Christian Ministry* with an emphasis in *Leadership.* As a leadership strategist and consultant, he conducts leadership seminars for churches, consults leaders, and speaks at conferences throughout the United States. He is recognized by his peers as a leadership specialist and a leader of leaders.

Contact Information

P. Ronald Wilder is available for consultation on various topics related to leadership, vision, teamwork, team building, mentoring, change, transition, etc. Those wishing to contact him for consultation, coaching, speaking engagements, conferences or for an *ABC's of Leadership* seminar may do so through:

P. Ronald Wilder Ministries
P.O. Box 100935
Birmingham, AL 35210
205-956-9672

info@pronaldwilder.com
or
www.pronaldwilder.com

Printed in the United States
By Bookmasters